Individualism

A READER

EDITED BY / George H. Smith
and Marilyn Moore

INTRODUCTION BY GEORGE H. SMITH

Library of Congress Cataloging-in-Publication Data

Individualism: a reader/edited by George H. Smith and Marilyn Moore; with an introduction by George H. Smith.
   pages cm.—(Libertarianism.org readers)
  Includes bibliographical references and index.
ISBN 978-1-939709-63-9 (pbk. : alk. paper)
1. Individualism. I. Smith, George H., 1949– editor.

B824.I525 2015
141'.4—dc23

                              2014049155

Printed in the United States of America.

CATO INSTITUTE
1000 Massachusetts Ave., N.W.
Washington, D.C. 20001
www.cato.org

Individualism

LIBERTARIANISM.ORG READERS

SERIES EDITOR
Aaron Ross Powell

INDIVIDUALISM

HERBERT SPENCER
(FORTHCOMING)

CRITICS OF STATE EDUCATION
(FORTHCOMING)

CONTENTS

PREFACE

This book is a collection of writings by defenders of individualism. Some major critics of individualism are discussed in the Introduction.

All selections ("documents") are in the public domain. Some of the writers included here, such as J. S. Mill and Oscar Wilde, are generally known, whereas others, such as Lysander Spooner and Auberon Herbert, are known mainly to libertarians. We have included some obscure authors, such as Henry Wilson, because we think their writings have considerable merit and deserve to be more widely read. A number of our selections have never appeared in previous anthologies. Therefore, even readers familiar with the literature on individualism will probably find something new in this Reader.

This is the first in a series of Readers to be published by Libertarianism.org. We wish to thank Aaron Powell of the Cato Institute for his support and encouragement. We also wish to thank Dr. Daniel E. Cullen and Mrs. Paula Bramsen Cullen of the Chicago-based Opportunity Foundation.

—GHS
—MM

INTRODUCTION

BY GEORGE H. SMITH

I

In 1840, in the second volume of *Democracy in America*, Alexis de Tocqueville said that "individualism" was "a word recently coined."[1] Similarly, 16 years later, in *The Old Régime and the French Revolution*, Tocqueville wrote:

> That word "individualism" . . . was unknown to our ancestors, for the good reason that in their days every individual necessarily belonged to a group and no one could regard himself as an isolated unit.[2]

As we shall see, "individualism" originated as a term of opprobrium, and it has retained its negative connotations to this day among both conservative and socialist intellectuals, whose criticisms have much in common. Because the selections in this anthology are devoted to defenses of individualism in its myriad forms, much of this introduction explains the major criticisms of individualism. For the sake of balance, I have frequently

---

[1] Alexis de Tocqueville, *Democracy in America*, ed. J. P. Mayer, trans. George Lawrence (Garden City: Anchor Books, 1969), 506.

[2] Alexis de Tocqueville, *The Old Régime and the French Revolution* [1856], trans. Stuart Gilbert (New York: Anchor Books, 1983), 96.

allowed critics to speak for themselves by quoting extensively from their writings.

Although it is not uncommon for critics to do less than full justice to the position they oppose, the ideas associated with individualism have been especially liable to this kind of abuse, which sometimes amounts to little more than political hucksterism. A recent example may be found in *The Myth of Individualism* by Peter L. Callero. Intended as an introduction to sociology, this book introduces students to the notion of individualism by invoking the notorious Unabomber, Theodore Kaczynski, who, between 1978 and 1995, murdered 3 people and injured 23 others. Why should a vicious serial killer be tagged as a representative of "extreme" individualism? Callero summarizes his reasons as follows:

> Kaczynski's extreme commitment to individualism is evident in (1) his intentional avoidance of personal relationships, (2) his deliberate physical separation from others, (3) the belief that he could live out his life completely independent of a larger community, (4) his solitary development of a personal program of social reform, and (5) his private strategy to unilaterally impose his ideas through a series of private acts that destroyed the lives of others.[3]

According to Callero, "Freedom of choice and self-determination are virtuous principles, but when selfish individual interests threaten to destroy the common good, the limits of individualism are exposed."[4]

Unfortunately but predictably, Callero is vague when it comes to defining "the common good"—a catchphrase with many

---

[3] Peter L. Callero, *The Myth of Individualism: How Social Forces Shape Our Lives* (Lanham, MD: Rowman & Littlefield, 2009), 18.
[4] Ibid., 19.

variations that has been used by murderous dictators throughout history. May we therefore say that the "common good," when pushed to extremes, results in the likes of Stalin and Hitler?

This comparison would be cheap theatrics, of course, but Callero does not hesitate to use the same tactic when criticizing individualism. In fact, if Theodore Kaczynski had not resorted to violence and murder, if instead he had respected the rights of other people to live their lives as they see fit—a principle that has always been essential to liberal individualism, even in its extreme manifestations—then his decision to live as an eccentric hermit would have had no effect whatsoever on the "common good." Thus, Callero's first four points are irrelevant to the supposedly harmful effects of even the most extreme individualism. Ayn Rand, for instance, was an extreme individualist by any standard, but because she vigorously defended the equal rights of individuals to be free from the initiation of physical force, she would not have served Callero's purpose of creating a caricature of individualism. Who, after all, will rally to the defense of the Unabomber?

I I

Callero is not the first critic of individualism, nor will he be the last, to equate "individualism" with physical isolation. Karl Marx made a similar point in his discussion of the "isolated individual" supposedly championed by Adam Smith and other classical liberals.

> The more deeply we go back into history, the more does the individual, and hence also the producing individual, appear as dependent, as belonging to a greater whole. . . . Only in the eighteenth century, in "civil society," do the various forms of social

connectedness confront the individual as a mere means towards his private purposes, as external necessity. But the epoch
which produces this standpoint, that of the isolated individual,
is also precisely that of the hitherto most developed social
(from this standpoint general) relations. The human being is
in the most literal sense a political animal, not merely a gregar-
ious animal, but an animal which can individuate itself only in
the midst of society. Production by an isolated individual outside society—a rare exception which may occur when a civilized
person in whom the social forces are already dynamically present is cast by accident into the wilderness—is as much of an absurdity as is the development of language without individuals
living *together* and talking to each other.[5]

Elsewhere, Marx wrote: "Man is not an abstract being, squat-
ting outside the world. Man is in the human world, the state, society."[6] Man is not an abstract being, and Marx objects to any
theory that treats him as such. But this abstract individual differs
altogether from the "isolated individual" to which Marx objected
in the passage quoted above.

The abstract individual has nothing in common with the isolated individual of Marx and other socialist critics of individualism. "Abstract" means that particular attributes have been
abstracted from real human beings and then integrated to form
a single concept. The term "isolated," however, means something
quite different: it refers to a person who lives apart from other
people, like Crusoe on his island.

---

[5] Karl Marx, *Grundrisse: Foundations of the Critique of Political Economy*, trans.
Martin Nicolaus (London: Penguin Books, 1993), 84.
[6] Karl Marx, "A Contribution to the Critique of Hegel's Philosophy of Right," in
Karl Marx: Early Writings, trans. Rodney Livingstone and Gregor Benton
(New York: Vintage Books, 1975), 244.

We should not confuse abstraction (a mental process) with isolation (a physical state). Liberal individualism, contrary to Marxian mythology, did not focus on man apart from his social environment. Quite the reverse is true. Man's sociability and social relations have been a central concern of individualists since the 17th century.[7]

In the final analysis, every social theory must employ some abstract concept of human beings. When Marx speaks of "man," he means not this or that particular man but man in general; he means not a concrete individual but an abstract individual. Social theorists may disagree with how to construct their theoretical models, but no theorist can dispense with models altogether. Marx made this very point about the notion of production.

> [A]ll epochs of production have certain common traits, common characteristics. *Production in general* is an abstraction, but a rational abstraction in so far as it really brings out and fixes the common element and thus saves us repetition.[8]

The abstract individual—otherwise known as "human nature"—is the foundation of social and political philosophy. We cannot generalize without it; we can only refer to particular human beings. We can say "Bob did this" or "Ted did that," but we cannot generalize. The abstract individual allows us to move from the particulars of history to the generalizations of theory. If a critic believes that a particular conception of the individual omits relevant characteristics, then he is objecting to a specific

---

[7] On this point generally, see George H. Smith, *The System of Liberty: Themes in the History of Classical Liberalism* (Cambridge: Cambridge University Press, 2013), especially chapter 9.
[8] Marx, *Grundrisse*, 85.

abstraction, not to the process of abstraction as such. In this case, the critic should offer an alternative conception of the abstract individual and argue for its acceptance.

I I I

Ironically perhaps, key elements in the Marxian criticism of individualism differ little from a popular conservative complaint (though the same point is typically used for different purposes). Consider this comment by Marx: "In this [individualistic] society of free competition, the individual appears detached from the natural bonds etc. which in earlier historical periods make him the accessory of a definite and limited human conglomerate."[9]

Similarly, from Edmund Burke to modern conservatives and neoconservatives, we hear that individualism leads to a destructive *social atomism* that ignores the social nature of human beings. According to Burke, if people view society as nothing more than a voluntary association for the pursuit of self-interest, while relying upon their "private stock of reason" to assess the desirability of traditional customs, values, and institutions, then the commonwealth will eventually "crumble away [and] be disconnected into the dust and powder of individuality."[10]

Writing in 1790, during the early stage of the French Revolution, Burke attacked the Constituent Assembly for abolishing the privileges of the nobility and the Catholic Church. Such measures were an effort to reduce all citizens to "one homogeneous mass."

---

[9] Ibid., 83.
[10] Edmund Burke, *Reflections on the Revolution in France* (Harmondsworth, Middlesex: Penguin Books, 1986), 194.

Whatever their abuses, those orders had served as "a strong barrier against the excesses of despotism." Without such intermediate powers to serve as buffers between the individual and the state, "the most completely arbitrary power that has ever appeared on earth" might very well arise.[11] To base a legal system on "an unsocial, uncivil, unconnected chaos of elementary principles,"[12] such as a theory of individual rights, is to pave the way for "anarchy." And out of the chaos of anarchy will inevitably emerge popular demand for a despotic leader with absolute power to restore social order. Thus did Burke, according to many of his admirers, foresee that the revolution would end in despotism, years before Napoleon's military dictatorship.

When Burke expressed his fear of a society consisting of "one homogenous mass," he sounded an alarm that has been sounded many times since, down to the present day, by conservatives in the European tradition. As the sociologist Robert Nisbet explained, conservative writers have used "masses" to mean "an aggregate discernible less by numbers than its lack of internal social structure, integrating tradition, and shared moral values." Nisbet continued: "One of the effects of the [French] Revolution's peculiar form of nihilism, Burke thought, was its effective desocializing of human beings, its atomizing of the population by virtue of its destructiveness toward traditional social bonds."[13]

> The idea of the mass developed and spread widely in the nineteenth century. It is strong in Tocqueville, who thought one of the great dangers of democracy was its creation of the mass in the

[11] Ibid., 300–301.
[12] Ibid., 195.
[13] Robert Nisbet, *Conservatism: Dream and Reality* (Minneapolis: University of Minnesota Press, 1986), 45.

first place—through emphasis upon the majority and through egalitarian values which tended to level populations—and then its increasing dependence on the mass, leading to a plebiscitary dictatorship. Burckhardt, Nietzsche and Kierkegaard, all wrote in apprehension of the coming of mass society and its desocializing effect upon the individual; an effect that would make government a combination of guardian and despot.[14]

The fear that a type of soft despotism would emerge out of a mass democratic society was famously expressed by Alexis de Tocqueville in *Democracy in America*. Tocqueville's depressing forecast is closely related to his concerns about individualism.

> Individualism is a calm and considered feeling which disposes each citizen to isolate himself from the mass of his fellows and withdraw into the circle of family and friends; with this little society formed to his taste, he gladly leaves the greater society to look after itself.[15]

Unlike the "depraved feeling" of egoism, which springs from blind instinct, individualism, argued Tocqueville, "is based on misguided judgment [and] inadequate understanding."[16] Over time, however, individualism tends to degenerate into pure egoism, because it ignores the civic virtues on which society depends. Individualism is a product of an egalitarian democracy that abolishes intermediate powers and thereby leaves the individual isolated and defenseless against the power of centralized government. This kind of despotism cannot take hold unless society has been fragmented into isolated atoms, and because egalitarian democracy promotes the social atomism of individ-

---

[14] Ibid., 46.
[15] Tocqueville, *Democracy in America,* 507.
[16] Ibid.

ualism, democracy and despotism "fatally complete and support each other."[17]

It is near the end of *Democracy in America* that we find Tocqueville's chilling vision of the possible future of individualism in an egalitarian democracy. His remarks deserve to be quoted at length.

> I want to imagine under what new features despotism could present itself to the world; I see an innumerable crowd of similar and equal men who spin around restlessly, in order to gain small and vulgar pleasures with which they fill their souls. Each one of them, withdrawn apart, is like a stranger to the destiny of all the others; his children and his particular friends form for him the entire human species; as for the remainder of his fellow citizens, he is next to them, but he does not see them; he touches them without feeling them; he exists only in himself and for himself alone, and if he still has a family, you can say that at least he no longer has a country.
>
> Above those men arises an immense and tutelary power that alone takes charge of assuring their enjoyment and of looking after their fate. It is absolute, detailed, regular, far-sighted and mild. It would resemble paternal power if, like it, it had as a goal to prepare men for manhood; but on the contrary it seeks only to fix them irrevocably in childhood; it likes the citizens to enjoy themselves, provided that they think only about enjoying themselves. It works willingly for their happiness; but it wants to be the unique agent for it and the sole arbiter; it attends to their security, provides for their needs, facilitates their pleasures, conducts their principal affairs, directs their industry, settles their estates, divides their inheritances; how can it not remove entirely from them the trouble to think and the difficulty of living?

---

[17] Ibid., 510.

This is how it makes the use of free will less useful and rarer every day; how it encloses the action of the will within a smaller space and little by little steals from each citizen even the use of himself. Equality has prepared men for all these things; it has disposed men to bear them and often even to regard them as a benefit.

After having thus taken each individual one by one into its powerful hands, and having molded him as it pleases, the sovereign power extends its arms over the entire society; it covers the surface of society with a network of small, complicated, minute, and uniform rules, which the most original minds and the most vigorous souls cannot break through to go beyond the crowd; it does not break wills, but it softens them, bends them and directs them; it rarely forces action, but it constantly opposes your acting; it does not destroy, it prevents birth; it does not tyrannize, it hinders, it represses, it enervates, it extinguishes, it stupefies, and finally it reduces each nation to being nothing more than a flock of timid and industrious animals, of which the government is the shepherd.[18]

Tocqueville did not regard this outcome as inevitable, nor did he long for the establishment of an aristocratic class or other privileged orders in America (or for their reinstatement in Europe). The hope for modern democracy lay in an independent judiciary and local liberties, but most especially in a free press and other voluntary associations. By merging individual interests into the common interest of an association, citizens may rely on a collective defense against state power: "Thenceforth they are no longer isolated individuals. . . ."

[18] Alexis de Tocqueville, *Democracy in America: Historical-Critical Edition of De la démocratie en Amérique*, vol. 4, ed. Eduardo Nolla, trans. James T. Schleifer. (Indianapolis: Liberty Fund, 2010). http://oll.libertyfund.org/titles/tocqueville-democracy-in-america-historical-critical-edition-vol-4#Tocqueville_1532–04_EN_1034.

Americans of all ages, stations in life, and all types of disposition are forever forming associations. There are not only commercial and industrial associations in which all take part, but others of a thousand different types—religious, moral, serious, futile, very general and very limited, immensely large and very minute. Americans combine to give fêtes, found seminaries, build churches, distribute books, and send missionaries to the antipodes. [I]f they want to proclaim a truth or propagate some feeling by the encouragement of a great example, they form an association. In every case, at the head of any new undertaking, where in France you would find the government or in England some territorial magnate, in the United States you are sure to find an association.[19]

Furthermore, Americans had embraced a theory that mitigated the deleterious effects of individualism, a theory that enabled them "to combine their own advantage with that of their fellow citizens." American moralists did not preach the beauty of self-sacrifice; they did not "pretend that one must sacrifice himself for his fellows because it is a fine thing to do." But they did believe in the utility of such virtues, that is, that a concern for the public good furthers each person's self-interest, rightly understood.

So the doctrine of self-interest properly understood is not new, but it is among the Americans of our time that it has come to be universally accepted. It has become popular. One finds it at the root of all actions. It is interwoven in all they say. You hear it as much from the poor as from the rich.[20]

It was for these and similar reasons that Tocqueville, who occasionally had favorable things to say about individualism,[21] did

---

[19] Tocqueville, *Democracy in America*, trans. Mayer, 516, 513.
[20] Ibid., 526.
[21] See, for example, *The Old Régime and the French Revolution*, 108, where Tocqueville refers to "a spirit of resistance and a sturdy individualism" that had prevented pre-revolutionary France from degenerating into a servile state.

not view democratic despotism as the inevitable outcome of American individualism. Tocqueville regarded social determinism as a "false and cowardly doctrine" that produced "feeble men and pusillanimous nations." Humanity is neither "entirely free or completely enslaved." Although our social environment sets limits on our actions, "within those vast limits man is strong and free, and so are peoples." In the final analysis, it is up to people themselves whether democratic equality will "lead to servitude or freedom, knowledge or barbarism, prosperity or wretchedness."

One of the most perceptive criticisms of *Democracy in America* by an American was written by Irish-born E. L. Godkin, who founded and edited *The Nation* and became known for his fierce opposition to American imperialism. A classical liberal who advocated limited government, free trade, and the gold standard, Godkin agreed with Tocqueville on a number of political issues, but he believed that Tocqueville's analysis of American individualism and democracy had been warped by the perspective of a European aristocrat. Although Godkin criticized *Democracy in America* on a number of levels—for one thing, he thought that Tocqueville's treatment was overly simplistic—his major criticism was that, contrary to Tocqueville, individualism was a cause, not an effect, of American democracy. Individualism, which ran deep in the American character, owed much to the demands of frontier living.

> [W]ith the assistance of steamboats and railways, and of immigration from Europe, the pioneering element in the population, the class devoted to the task of creating new political and social organizations as distinguished from that engaged in perfecting old ones, assumed a great preponderance. It spread itself thinly over a vast area of soil, of such extraordinary fertility that a very

slight amount of toil expended on it affords returns that might have satisfied even the dreams of Spanish avarice. The result has been very much what we might have concluded, *a priori*, that it would be. A society composed at the period of its formation mainly of young men, coming from all parts of the world in quest of fortune, released from the ordinary restraints of family, church, and public opinion, even of the civil law, naturally and inevitably acquires a certain contempt for authority and impatience of it, and individualism among them develops very rapidly. If you place this society, thus constituted, in the midst of a wilderness, where each member of it has to contend, tools in hand, with Nature herself for wealth, or even subsistence, the ties which bind him to his fellow will for a while at least be rarely anything stronger than that of simple contiguity. The only mutual obligation which this relation suggests is that of rendering assistance occasionally in overcoming material difficulties—in other words, the simplest bond which can unite human beings. Each person is, from the necessity of the case, so absorbed in his own struggle for existence, that he has seldom occasion or time for the consideration and cultivation of his social relations. He knows nothing of the antecedents of his neighbors, nor they of his. They are not drawn together, in all probability, by a single memory or association. They have drifted into the same locality, it is true, under the guidance of a common impulse, and this a selfish one. So that the settler gets into the habit of looking at himself as an individual, of contemplating himself and his career separate and apart from his social organization. We do not say that this breeds selfishness—far from it; but it breeds individualism.[22]

---

[22] Edwin Lawrence Godkin, "Aristocratic Opinions of Democracy," in *Problems of Modern Democracy: Political and Economic Essays*, 3rd ed. (New York: Charles Scribner's Sons, 1898), 38–39.

Yehoshua Arieli has nicely contrasted the views of Tocqueville and Godkin:

> The difference between the views of the two authors lay not only in the causal relationship between individualism and democracy, but in Godkin's emphatic statement that individualism was a fundamental character trait of the American. It expressed itself in self-reliance, abundant energy of action, ideals of unrestrained individual freedom, the capacity for organization and daring enterprise, and the belief in a free competitive economy. As against Tocqueville's view that its free institutions and enlightened self-interest had defeated individualism in America, Godkin concluded that both rested on the vigor of American individualism. Godkin's evaluation revealed the degree to which Americans had accepted the concept of individualism as a basic character trait of their society in the years since Tocqueville's analysis.[23]

I V

The word "individualism" may have been coined during the 1820s by the French theocrat and anti-revolutionary Joseph de Maistre, who assailed the diversity of religious and political opinions that had supplanted the relative uniformity of pre-revolutionary France. According to Maistre, this "absolute individualism," this "infinite fragmentation" of doctrines, was dangerous because it had shattered the religious consensus essential to peace and social harmony. Europe had lost its moral bearings "because there was too much liberty in Europe and not enough Religion." The ultimate cause of this disaster was the

---

[23] Yehoshua Arieli, *Individualism and Nationalism in American Ideology* (Cambridge, MA: Harvard University Press, 1964), 200–201.

Protestant Reformation and its defense of freedom of conscience, a teaching that had resulted in a "deep and frightening division of minds."

Only the restoration of the Catholic Church to its position of authority, backed by an absolute monarchy, could remedy the disastrous effects of "political protestantism." Nine years later, the theocrat Hugues Felicité-de Lamennais issued a similar warning: The same individualism that causes "anarchy among minds" will inevitably produce political anarchy and thereby overturn the "very basis of human society." Individualism, according to Lamennais, is "power without obedience" and "law without duty."[24]

A similar critic of individualism, Louis-Gabriel-Ambroise de Bonald, was able to implement some of his policies while working for government during the Bourbon Restoration.

> In 1827, Charles X put Bonald, a convinced opponent of freedom of the press, in charge of censorship. More important than these posts, however, was his role as a member of the Chamber of Deputies from 1815 to 1823. There he helped to lead the Ultra-Royalist Party and enjoyed his greatest success with the repeal of legal divorce in December 1815. He was also the guiding spirit behind other Ultra-Royalist policies, such as the attempt to restore trade guilds and the practice of primogeniture and entail for landed property.[25]

[24] See the quotations in Steven Lukes, *Individualism* (Oxford: Basil Blackwell, 1973), 4; also Robert Nisbet, "Conservatism," in *A History of Sociological Analysis*, ed. Tom Bottomore and Robert Nisbet (New York: Basic Books, 1978), 80–117. Although I have some disagreements with Lukes, his short book is an indispensable source on the various meanings of "individualism" and their histories.

[25] Christopher Olaf Blum, "Introduction," in *Critics of the Enlightenment: Readings in the French Counter-Revolutionary Tradition*, ed. and trans. Christopher Olaf Blum (Wilmington, DE: ISI Books, 2004), xxvii.

In 1843, the militant Catholic conservative Louis Veuillot put his objections to individualism this way:

> The evil which plagues France is not unknown; everyone agrees in giving it the same name: *individualism.*
>
> It is not difficult to see that a country where individualism reigns is not long in the normal condition of society, since society is the union of minds and interests, and individualism is division carried to the infinite degree.
>
> All for each, each for all, that is society; each for himself, and thus each against all, that is individualism.[26]

The following passage by Philippe Bénéton captures the essential ideas of the early conservative critics of individualism.

> To the myth of autonomy, [counter-revolutionary thought] responds that the man of the radical version of modernity, the perfectly autonomous man, is a fiction. The French counter-revolutionaries, after Aristotle, Saint Thomas, and Burke, ceaselessly insisted, with arguments difficult to refute, upon the social dimension of human existence. Man does not make himself by himself; he receives from others (his relatives, his contemporaries, past generations) much more than he gives. Man does not live alone; he has a deep, fundamental need for others because he is a being constituted by his relations. He who would exercise autonomous judgment in fact relies upon a thousand things he takes on the authority of others: that the earth is round, that Napoleon existed, that his parents are his parents, and so on. He who would attempt to live in an individualistic manner leaves behind him ties that matter, particularly those of the heart. Full and complete autonomy is a dream and a pernicious one at that. . . . Modern individualism loosens social ties, which are ties of attachment, in favor of contractual and utilitarian relations. Solid attachments are those which are

---

[26] Quoted in Lukes, *Individualism*, 9.

created in the midst of communities, whether they be familial, religious, local, political, or professional communities. A good society cannot be reduced to a collection of individuals.[27]

A key aspect of this perspective, Bénéton points out, was "the rejection of the sovereignty of the individual with the affirmation of the rights of conscience."[28] Liberty of conscience, which many Catholic conservatives blamed on the Protestant Reformation (and, later, the Enlightenment), had brought about the fragmentation of religious doctrines, and this in turn had destroyed the uniformity of belief on which social order depends. Religious diversity was followed by a diversity of political opinions, including radical ideas about individual rights and government by consent—and from there it was a short, logical step to the revolutionary upheavals of 18th-century Europe. Only a restoration of religious and political authorities, a system in which ordinary people defer to their superiors, can counteract the corrosive individualism of modern times.

The term "individualism" was also used in the mid-1820s by the disciples of Saint Simon. For the Saint-Simonians, as for their theocratic contemporaries, "individualism" was a term of opprobrium, one that characterized the Enlightenment stress on political liberalism, freedom of conscience, individual rights, and the pursuit of economic self-interest. According to the Saint-Simonians, the Enlightenment defenders of individualism, in reviving the egoism of Epicurus and the Stoics, and in upholding the right of individual judgment, had denied the legitimacy of

[27] Philippe Bénéton, "Foreword," in *Critics of the Enlightenment: Readings in the French Counter-Revolutionary Tradition*, ed. and trans. Christopher Olaf Blum (Wilmington, DE: ISI Books, 2004), xi.
[28] Ibid., xiv.

any authoritative organization that sought to direct the moral interests of humanity. This passage from the chief manifesto of the Saint-Simonians is typical:

> [T]he last organic period offers a valuable subject for observation in the works of those barbaric times before feudalism was firmly established. At that time there existed a spirit of individualism and of egoism similar to that dominating our industrialists today. The principle of competition, of liberty, reigned not only among the warriors of different countries, but within the same country among the warriors of different provinces, cantons, towns and castles. In our time, too, the principle of competition, of liberty, and of war exists among the merchants and manufacturers of the same country. It exists between province and province, between town and town, between factory and factory, and, we may add, between shop and shop.[29]

V

Having covered some traditional objections to individualism, we shall now turn to some historical reflections by important historians of individualism. As before, and in keeping with the spirit of this Reader, I shall quote at length in many cases rather than paraphrase. I do this in the hope that students and others unfamiliar with the secondary literature will be motivated to consult the originals. Of course, this topic is so complex and the literature so vast that I can only discuss a handful of the historical

---

[29] *The Doctrine of Saint-Simon: An Exposition, First Year, 1828–1829*, trans. Georg G. Iggers (Boston: Beacon Press, 1958), 99.

accounts, and those in a cursory manner. (For a more extensive list of secondary accounts, see the list of Recommended Reading at the end of this volume.)

I shall begin, as many historians do, with the classic book by the Swiss historian Jacob Burckhardt, *The Civilization of the Renaissance in Italy* (1860). Although widely admired as the pioneering work in its field, this book has also been severely criticized. It is not my purpose either to defend or criticize Burckhardt's famous thesis about the origins of individuality. Rather, after sketching his thesis, I briefly consider some problems with the notion of "individuality," which differs substantially from sundry types of "individualism."

In the chapter titled "The Development of the Individual," Jacob Burckhardt wrote:

In the Middle Ages both sides of human consciousness—that which was turned within as that which was turned without—lay dreaming or half awake beneath a common veil. The veil was woven of faith, illusion and childish prepossession, through which the world and history were seen as clad in strange hues. Man was conscious of himself only as a member of a race, people, party, family or corporation—only through some general category. In Italy this veil first melted into air; an *objective* treatment and consideration of the state and of all the things of this world became possible. The *subjective* side at the same time asserted itself with corresponding emphasis; man became a *spiritual* individual, and recognized himself as such. . . .

In far earlier times we can here and there detect a development of free personality. . . . But at the close of the thirteenth century Italy began to swarm with individuality; the ban laid upon human personality was dissolved; and a thousand figures meet us each in its own special shape and dress. . . . The Italians of the fourteenth century knew little of false modesty in any shape; not one of them was afraid of singularity, of being and seeming unlike his neighbors.[30]

Burckhardt attributed this awakening and heightened sense of individuality to "the political circumstances of Italy." Specifically, the despotism of the various city-states "fostered in the highest degree the individuality not only of the tyrant or *condottiere* himself, but also of the men whom he protected or used as his tools—the secretary, minister, poet and companion." Petty tyrants came and went in quick succession, so those in power learned to enjoy themselves while they could, seeking "to obtain the greatest satisfaction from a possibly very brief period of power and influence."[31] And this typically involved the flaunting of one's individuality.

Even those Italians who were barred from the corridors of power did not find political servitude a barrier to individuality, "for political impotence does not hinder the different tendencies and manifestations of private life from thriving in the fullest vigor and variety." The considerable individual freedom of the city-states, along with a church that did not severely interfere with municipal governments, "undoubtedly favored the growth of individual thought."[32] Indeed, when despotism made participation in civic life impossible, many people became indifferent to politics and pursued the pleasures of private life instead.

When reading a classic work in history (or in any other field), we may be tempted to let key words wash over us without examining them closely. This is especially true with cultural histories

---

[30] Jacob Burckhardt, *The Civilization of the Renaissance in Italy*, trans. S. G. C. Middlemore (London: Penguin Books, 1990), 98.
[31] Ibid., 99.
[32] Ibid.

of the sort that Burckhardt wrote, in which the ambiguities and imprecisions of subjective perceptions and preferences are in the nature of the beast. That Burckhardt, one of the most accomplished historians of his time, was well aware of this problem is evident from his description of his great book as an "essay in the strictest sense." "To each eye," he wrote, "the outlines of a given civilization present a different picture"; and "the same studies which have served for this work might easily, in other hands, not only receive a wholly different treatment and application, but lead also to essentially different conclusions."[33]

With this proviso, let us consider Burckhardt's conception of individuality. This concept is obviously not related to political or economic individualism, because individuality, as Burckhardt used the term, grew from systems of petty despotism throughout Italy. As he noted in an earlier chapter, 14th-century Florence was "the scene of the richest development of human individuality, while for the despots no other individuality could be suffered to live and thrive but their own and that of their nearest dependents."[34]

Individuality, for Burckhardt, signifies focused attention on the inner self and a positive evaluation of the unique features of one's personality. When Burckhardt wrote about "a development of free personality" and a dissolution of "the ban laid upon human personality," he was referring to an atmosphere of "cultural liberalism" in which exhibitions of personal differences and eccentricities were not only tolerated but actually prized. This kind of individuality, however, may amount to nothing more than vain egotism. Even the most superficial and boring petty

---

[33] Quoted by Peter Burke in the "Introduction" to ibid., 5.
[34] Ibid., 25.

despot in Renaissance Italy could prance about and display his individuality in this sense, secure in the knowledge that his power and wealth would shield him from overt public ridicule. Far more important—and this is really the substance of Burckhardt's book—was the profound individualism (not merely individuality) exhibited in Renaissance art and literature.

A serious problem with any historical work that deals with an age and culture different from our own is that we cannot fully understand and appreciate the subjective world of the proverbial common man. In many instances, we must settle for records of what the literate class believed—more specifically, those members of that class with sufficient time and resources to record their thoughts in writing or in some form of art. Nevertheless, we do what we can, and our chief resource here is introspection. This is where we may encounter a problem with Burckhardt's claim that during the Middle Ages, "Man was conscious of himself *only* . . . through some general category." Is this credible? Are we to believe that the typical person in the Middle Ages had no sense of his own distinctive personality or of the personalities of others? The relevant point here, as indicated previously, would seem to be that only in some historical circumstances have individualizing characteristics been socially valued as much as (or more than) one's membership in a particular social class or group. The following remarks by Aaron Gurevich are illuminating in this regard. Regarding the thesis of Colin Morris that the "discovery of the individual" may be traced to the 12th century, Gurevich writes:

> It would be wrong to confuse interest in "the inner landscape of the individual" (the discovery of self) with the "discovery of the individual." While stressing the seriousness of intention in discussion of ethical problems, Abelard and other authors of the twelfth century at the same time . . . felt a need to classify various

"estates" and "vocations." They write of individuals as types or models.... "Likeness" was a fundamental theological category in the twelfth century, and the self-modification of the individual took place in a context defined by models—Christ, the Apostles, the Patriarchs, the Saints and the Church.... No mention was made at that period of anything like a personal lifestyle. It was not until the following century that the individual and the group began to grow apart.[35]

The objections of Gurevich (and other scholars) notwithstanding, the classic book by Colin Morris, *The Discovery of the Individual 1050–1200*, remains one of the most interesting historical treatments of individualism ever written. According to Morris, modern individualism emerged during the "twelfth-century Renaissance," not (as Burckhardt claimed) from the later and better-known Italian Renaissance. The 12th century witnessed "a new respect for man and human possibilities.... There is a rapid rise in individualism and humanism in the years from about 1080 to 1150."[36] The following passages give us a sense of Morris's perspective.

> This book will not be concerned with the origins of ... political individualism, but with individualism at a more directly personal level: with that respect for individual human beings, their character and opinion, which has been instilled into us by our cultural tradition, and with its implications for personal relationships and beliefs. The hard core of this individualism lies in the psychological experience ... of a clear distinction between my being, and that of other people. The significance of this experience is greatly

[35] Aaron Gurevich, *The Origins of European Individualism*, trans. Katharine Judelson (Oxford, U.K.: Blackwell Publishers, 1995), 8.
[36] Colin Morris, *The Discovery of the Individual 1050–1200* (Toronto: University of Toronto Press, 1987), 7.

increased by our belief in the *value* of human beings in themselves. Humanism may not be the same thing as individualism . . . but they are at least first cousins, for a respect for the dignity of man is naturally accompanied by a respect for individual men. . . .

Europe has developed literary forms specially devoted to the exploration of the individual and his relationships, such as biography, autobiography, and the novel; forms which are unknown, or relatively undeveloped, in other cultures. . . . There has . . . been in Western literature a strong element of self-discovery, expressed in highly personal lyric poetry or in the stress of personal experience in religion. This "inwardness" or acute self-awareness has been a distinctive feature of Western man.[37]

Unlike many accounts that stress the secular aspects of individualism, Morris maintains that Christianity contributed a great deal to its rise.

It is at once obvious that the Western view of the value of the individual owes a great deal to Christianity. A sense of individual identity and value is implicit in belief in a God who has called each man by name, who has sought him out as a shepherd seeks his lost sheep. Self-awareness and a serious concern with inner character is encouraged by the conviction that the believer must lay himself open to God, and be remade by the Holy Spirit. From the beginning, Christianity showed itself to be an "interior" religion. It also contains a strong element of respect for humanity. Its central belief, that God became man for man's salvation, is itself an affirmation of human dignity which could hardly be surpassed, and its principal ethical precept is that a man must love others as he loves himself. The value of the individual and the dignity of man are both written large in the pages of the Scriptures. It is understandable that in the centuries before 1100

---

[37] Ibid., 3–4.

these convictions had made only a limited impact upon the primitive society of western Europe. It depended largely upon tradition, and therefore could give little scope to the individual, and, as we shall see later, social conditions were not such as to encourage a high view of human dignity. Yet, even in these unfavorable circumstances, the Church had maintained at least a silent witness to the humanist elements in the gospel. . . . Ultimately a Christian origin can be found for many of the elements in the European concept of the self.[38]

VI

We have divided the selections for this Reader into six categories: Individuality, Social Individualism, Moral Individualism, Political Individualism, Religious Individualism, and Economic Individualism. The criteria for some of those categories, such as political and religious individualism, are fairly clear, whereas the boundaries of other categories, such as social and moral individualism, are indistinct. Even more troublesome is the problem of how some of the selections should be classified. The opening selections by Humboldt and Mill, for instance, cover so much ground that they could have been placed in any of the first three categories, so if there is logic in placing them under Individuality, it is a fuzzy logic indeed. Frankly, the deciding factor in some cases was the desire for balance among the sections. The brief introductions to the selections may help explain our reasoning.

[38] Ibid., 10–11.

One subject that we do not cover is methodological individualism. Those with an interest in this controversial and rather technical topic may wish to read my treatment in chapter 10 ("Methodological Individualism") of my book, *The System of Liberty: Themes in the History of Classical Liberalism*, published by Cambridge University Press in 2013.

PART ONE

INDIVIDUALITY

1. "OF THE INDIVIDUAL MAN, AND THE HIGHEST ENDS OF HIS EXISTENCE"

WILHELM VON HUMBOLDT

Chapter 2 of *The Sphere and Duties of Government*, trans. Joseph Coulthard (London: John Chapman, 1859)

Wilhelm von Humboldt (1767–1835) was a German man of letters and educator who made significant contributions to linguistics. After Humboldt finished writing The Sphere and Duties of Government *(titled* The Proper Sphere of Government *in a later translation) in 1792, some chapters were printed in a German periodical. A complete German edition did not appear until 1852, followed by an English translation that was published in 1854 by the English freethinker and libertarian John Chapman. The English version influenced J. S. Mill, who quoted from it in* On Liberty. *As Mill would later do, Humboldt argues that freedom and cultural diversity are essential to the development of individuality, which, in turn, is essential to happiness.*

The true end of Man, or that which is prescribed by the eternal and immutable dictates of reason, and not suggested by vague and transient desires, is the highest and most harmonious development of his powers to a complete and consistent whole. Freedom is the grand and indispensable condition which the possibility of such a development presupposes; but there is besides another essential,—intimately connected with freedom, it is true,—a variety of situations. Even the most free and self-reliant of men is thwarted and hindered in his development by uniformity of position. But as it is evident, on the one hand, that such a diversity is a constant result of freedom, and on the other, that there is a species of oppression which, without imposing restrictions on man himself, gives a peculiar impress of its own to surrounding circumstances; these two conditions, of freedom and variety of situation, may be regarded, in a certain sense, as one and the same. Still, it may contribute to perspicuity to point out the distinction between them.

Every human being, then, can act with but one force at the same time: or rather, our whole nature disposes us at any given time to some single form of spontaneous activity. It would therefore seem to follow from this, that man is inevitably destined to a partial cultivation, since he only enfeebles his energies by directing them to a multiplicity of objects. But we see the fallacy of such a conclusion when we reflect, that man has it in his power to avoid this one-sideness, by striving to unite the separate faculties of his nature, often singly exercised; by bringing into spontaneous co-operation, at each period of his life, the gleams of activity about to expire, and those which the future alone will kindle into living effulgence; and endeavouring to increase and diversify the powers with which he works, by harmoniously combining them, instead of looking for a mere variety of objects for their separate exercise. That which is effected, in the case of the individual, by the union of the past and future with the present, is produced in society by the mutual co-operation of its different single members; for, in all the stages of his existence, each individual can exhibit but one of those perfections only, which represent the possible features of human character. It is through such social union, therefore, as is based on the internal wants and capacities of its members, that each is enabled to participate in the rich collective resources of all the others. The experience of all, even the rudest, nations, furnishes us an example of a union thus formative of individual character, in the union of the sexes. And, although in this case the expression, as well of the difference as of the longing for union, appears more marked and striking, it is still no less active in other kinds of association where there is actually no difference of sex; it is only more difficult to discover in these, and may perhaps be more powerful for that very reason. If we were to follow out this idea, it might perhaps conduct us to a clearer insight into the phenomena of those unions so much in vogue among the ancients, and more especially the Greeks, among whom we find them countenanced even by the legislators themselves: I mean those so frequently, but unworthily, classed under the general appellation of ordinary love, and sometimes, but always erroneously, designated as mere friendship. The efficiency of all such unions as instruments of cultivation, wholly depends on the degree in which the component members can succeed in combining their personal independence with the intimacy of the common bond; for whilst, without this intimacy, one individual cannot sufficiently possess himself, as it were, of the nature of the others, independence is no less essential, in order that the perceived be assimilated into the being of the perceiver. Now, it is clear (to apply these conclusions to the respective conditions for culture,— freedom, and a variety of situations), that, on the one hand, individual energy is essential to the perceived and perceiver, into which social unions may be resolved; and, on the other, a difference between them, neither so great as to prevent the one from comprehending the other, nor so inconsiderable as to exclude admiration for that which the other possesses, and the desire of assimilating it into the perceiver's character.

This individual vigour, then, and manifold diversity, combine themselves in *originality*; and hence, that on which the consummate grandeur of our nature ultimately depends,—that towards which every human being must ceaselessly direct his efforts, and on which especially those who design to influence their fellow men must ever keep their eyes, is the *Individuality of Power and Development.* Just as this individuality springs naturally from the perfect freedom of action, and the greatest diversity in the agents, it tends immediately to produce them in turn. Even inanimate nature, which, proceeding in accordance with unchangeable laws, advances by regular grades of progression, appears more individual to the man who has been developed in his individuality. He transports himself, as it were, into the very centre of nature; and it is true, in the highest sense, that each still perceives the beauty and rich abundance of the outer world, in the exact measure in which he is conscious of their existence in his own soul. How much sweeter and closer must this correspondence become between effect and cause,—this reaction between internal feeling and outward perception,—when man is not only passively open to external sensations and impressions, but is himself also an agent!

If we attempt to confirm these principles by a closer application of them to the nature of the individual man, we find that everything which enters into the latter, reduces itself to the two elements of Form and Substance. The purest form, beneath the most delicate veil, we call Idea; the crudest substance, with the most imperfect form, we call sensuous Perception. Form springs from the union of substance. The richer and more various the substance that is united, the more sublime is the resulting form. A child of the gods is the offspring only of immortal parents: and as the blossom swells and ripens into fruit, and from the tiny germ imbedded in its soft pulp the new stalk shoots forth, laden with newly-clustering buds; so does the Form become in turn the substance of a still more exquisite Form. The intensity of power, moreover, increases in proportion to the greater variety and delicacy of the substance; since the internal cohesion increases with these. The substance seems as if blended in the form, and the form merged in the substance. Or, to speak without metaphor, the richer a man's feelings become in ideas, and his ideas in feelings, the more lofty and transcendent his sublimity; for upon this constant intermingling of form and substance, or of diversity with the individual unity, depends the perfect inter-fusion of the two natures which co-exist in man, and upon this, his greatness. But the force of the generation depends upon the energy of the generating forces. The consummating point of human existence is the flowering of these forces. In the vegetable world, the simple and less graceful form of the fruit seems to pre-figure the more perfect bloom and symmetry of the flower which it precedes, and which it is destined gradually to unfold. Every-thing conspires to the beautiful consummation of the blossom. That which first shoots forth from the little germ is not nearly so exquisite and fascinating. The full thick trunk, the broad leaves rapidly detaching themselves from each other, seem to require some fuller and fairer development; as the eye glances up the ascending stem, it marks the spiring grades of this development; more tender leaflets seem longing to unite themselves, and draw closer and closer together, until the central calyx of the crowning flower seems to give the sweet satisfaction to this growing desire. But destiny has not blessed the tribe of plants in this the law and process of their growth. The flower fades and dies, and the germ of the fruit reproduces the stem, as rude and unfinished as the former, to ascend slowly through the same stages of development as before. But when, in man, the blossom fades away, it is only to give place to another still more exquisitely beautiful; and the charm of the last and loveliest is only hidden from our view in the endlessly receding vistas of an inscrutable eternity. Now, whatever man receives externally, is only as the grain of seed. It is his own active energy alone that can convert the germ of the fairest growth, into a full and precious blessing for himself. It leads to beneficial issues only when it is full of vital power and essentially individual. The highest ideal, therefore, of the co-existence of human beings, seems to me to consist in a union in which each strives to develope himself from his own inmost nature, and for his own sake. The requirements of our physical and moral being would, doubtless, bring men together into communities; and even as the conflicts of warfare are more honourable than the fights of the arena, and the struggles of exasperated citizens more glorious than the hired and unsympathizing efforts of mere mercenaries, so would the exerted powers of such spontaneous agents succeed in eliciting the highest and noblest energies.

And is it not exactly this which so unspeakably captivates us in contemplating the life of Greece and Rome, and which in general captivates any age whatever in the contemplation of a remoter one? Is it not that these men had harder struggles to endure with the ruthless force of destiny, and harder struggles with their fellow men? that greater and more original energy and individuality constantly encountered each other, and gave rise in the encounter to ever new and beautiful forms? Every later epoch,—and in what a rapid course of declension must this now proceed!—is necessarily inferior in variety to that which it succeeded: in variety of nature,—the boundless forests have been cleared, the vast morasses dried up; in variety of human life, by the ever-increasing intercommunication and union of all human establishments. It is in this we find one of the chief causes which render the idea of the new, the uncommon, the marvelous, so much more rare,—which make affright or astonishment almost a disgrace,—and not only render the discovery of fresh and, till now, unknown expedients, far less necessary, but also all sudden, unpremeditated and urgent decisions. For, partly, the pressure of outward circumstances is less violent, while man is provided with more ample means for opposing them; partly, this resistance is no longer possible with the simple forces which nature bestows on all alike, fit for immediate application; and, in fine, partly a higher and more extended knowledge renders inventions less necessary, and the very increase of learning serves to blunt the edge of discovery. It is, on the other hand, undeniable that, whereas physical variety has so vastly declined, it has been succeeded by an infinitely richer and more satisfying intellectual and moral variety, and that our superior refinement can recognize more delicate differences and gradations, and our disciplined and susceptible character, if not so firmly consolidated as that of the ancients, can transfer them into the practical conduct of life,—differences and gradations which might have wholly escaped the notice of the sages of antiquity, or at least would have been discernible by them alone. To the human family at large, the same has happened as to the individual: the ruder features have faded away, the finer only have remained. And in view of this sacrifice of energy from generation to generation, we might regard it as a blessed dispensation if the whole human species were as one man; or the living force of one age could be transmitted to the succeeding one, along with its books and inventions. But this is far from being the case. It is true that our refinement possesses a peculiar force of its own, perhaps even surpassing the former in strength, just in proportion to the measure of its refinement; but it is a question whether the prior development, through the more robust and vigorous stages, must not always be the antecedent transition. Still, it is certain that the sensuous element in our nature, as it is the earliest germ, is also the most vivid expression of the spiritual.

While this is not the place, however, to enter on the discussion of this point, we are justified in concluding, from the other considerations we have urged, that we must at least preserve, with the most eager solicitude, all the force and individuality we may yet possess, and cherish aught that can tend in any way to promote them.

I therefore deduce, as the natural inference from what has been argued, *that reason cannot desire for man any other condition than that in which each individual not only enjoys the most absolute freedom of developing himself by his own energies, in his perfect individuality, but in which external nature even is left unfashioned by any human agency, but only receives the impress given to it by each individual of himself and his own free will, according to the measure of his wants and instincts, and restricted only by the limits of his powers and his rights.*

From this principle it seems to me, that Reason must never yield aught save what is absolutely required to preserve it. It must therefore be the basis of every political system, and must especially constitute the starting-point of the inquiry which at present claims our attention.

2. "OF INDIVIDUALITY, AS ONE OF THE ELEMENTS OF WELL-BEING"

JOHN STUART MILL

Chapter III of *On Liberty*, 2nd ed. (London: John Parker and Sons, 1859)

The Englishman J. S. Mill (1806–73) was one of the most influential philosophers of the 19th century. Educated by his father, the Scotsman James Mill (a protégé of Jeremy Bentham), John popularized the moral and political philosophy known as "utilitarianism." The following chapter is from Mill's celebrated book, On Liberty *(1859). His other works include* A System of Logic *(1843),* Principles of Political Economy *(1848),* Utilitarianism *(1863), and* On the Subjection of Women *(1869).*

Such being the reasons which make it imperative that human beings should be free to form opinions, and to express their opinions without reserve; and such the baneful consequences to the intellectual, and through that to the moral nature of man, unless this liberty is either conceded, or asserted in spite of prohibition; let us next examine whether the same reasons do not require that men should be free to act upon their opinions—to carry these out in their lives, without hindrance, either physical or moral, from their fellow-men, so long as it is at their own risk and peril. This last proviso is of course indispensable. No one pretends that actions should be as free as opinions. On the contrary, even opinions lose their immunity, when the circumstances in which they are expressed are such as to constitute their expression a positive instigation to some mischievous act. An opinion that corn-dealers are starvers of the poor, or that private property is robbery, ought to be unmolested when simply circulated through the press, but may justly incur punishment when delivered orally to an excited mob assembled before the house of a corn-dealer, or when handed about among the same mob in the form of a placard. Acts, of whatever kind, which, without justifiable cause, do harm to others, may be, and in the more important cases absolutely require to be, controlled by the unfavourable sentiments, and, when needful, by the active interference of mankind. The liberty of the individual must be thus far limited; he must not make himself a nuisance to other people. But if he refrains from molesting others in what concerns them, and merely acts according to his own inclination and judgment in things which concern himself, the same reasons which show that opinion should be free, prove also that he should be allowed, without molestation, to carry his opinions into practice at his own cost. That mankind are not infallible; that their truths, for the most part, are only half-truths; that unity of opinion, unless resulting from the fullest and freest comparison of opposite opinions, is not desirable, and diversity not an evil, but a good, until mankind are much more capable than at present of recognizing all sides of the truth, are principles applicable to men's modes of action, not less than to their opinions. As it is useful that while mankind are imperfect there should be different opinions, so is it that there should be different experiments of living; that free scope should be given to varieties of character, short of injury to others; and that the worth of different modes of life should be proved practically, when any one thinks fit to try them. It is desirable, in short, that in things which do not primarily concern others, individuality should assert itself. Where, not the person's own character, but the traditions or customs of other people are the rule of conduct, there is wanting one of the principal ingredients of human happiness, and quite the chief ingredient of individual and social progress.

In maintaining this principle, the greatest difficulty to be encountered does not lie in the appreciation of means towards an acknowledged end, but in the indifference of persons in general to the end itself. If it were felt that the free development of individuality is one of the leading essentials of well-being; that it is not only a coordinate element with all that is designated by the terms civilization, instruction, education, culture, but is itself a necessary part and condition of all those things; there would be no danger that liberty should be undervalued, and the adjustment of the boundaries between it and social control would present no extraordinary difficulty. But the evil is, that individual spontaneity is hardly recognized by the common modes of thinking, as having any intrinsic worth, or deserving any regard on its own account. The majority, being satisfied with the ways of mankind as they now are (for it is they who make them what they are), cannot comprehend why those ways should not be good enough for everybody; and what is more, spontaneity forms no part of the ideal of the majority of moral and social reformers, but is rather looked on with jealousy, as a troublesome and perhaps rebellious obstruction to the general acceptance of what these reformers, in their own judgment, think would be best for mankind. Few persons, out of Germany, even comprehend the meaning of the doctrine which Wilhelm Von Humboldt, so eminent both as a savant and as a politician, made the text of a treatise—that "the end of man, or that which is prescribed by the eternal or immutable dictates of reason, and not suggested by vague and transient desires, is the highest and most harmonious development of his powers to a complete and consistent whole;" that, therefore, the object "towards which every human being must ceaselessly direct his efforts, and on which especially those who design to influence their fellow-men must ever keep their eyes, is the individuality of power and development;" that for this there are two requisites, "freedom, and a variety of situations;" and that from the union of these arise "individual vigour and manifold diversity," which combine themselves in "originality."

Little, however, as people are accustomed to a doctrine like that of Von Humboldt, and surprising as it may be to them to find so high a value attached to individuality, the question, one must nevertheless think, can only be one of degree. No one's idea of excellence in conduct is that people should do absolutely nothing but copy one another. No one would assert that people ought not to put into their mode of life, and into the conduct of their concerns, any impress whatever of their own judgment, or of their own individual character. On the other hand, it would be absurd to pretend that people ought to live as if nothing whatever had been known in the world before they came into it; as if experience had as yet done nothing towards showing that one mode of existence, or of conduct, is preferable to another. Nobody denies that people should be so taught and trained in youth, as to know and benefit by the ascertained results of human experience. But it is the privilege and proper condition of a human being, arrived at the maturity of his faculties, to use and interpret experience in his own way. It is for him to find out what part of recorded experience is properly applicable to his own circumstances and character. The traditions and customs of other people are, to a certain extent, evidence of what their experience has taught them; presumptive evidence, and as such, have a claim to his deference:

but, in the first place, their experience may be too narrow; or they may not have interpreted it rightly. Secondly, their interpretation of experience may be correct, but unsuitable to him. Customs are made for customary circumstances, and customary characters; and his circumstances or his character may be uncustomary. Thirdly, though the customs be both good as customs, and suitable to him, yet to conform to custom, merely as custom, does not educate or develope in him any of the qualities which are the distinctive endowment of a human being. The human faculties of perception, judgment, discriminative feeling, mental activity, and even moral preference, are exercised only in making a choice. He who does anything because it is the custom, makes no choice. He gains no practice either in discerning or in desiring what is best. The mental and moral, like the muscular powers, are improved only by being used. The faculties are called into no exercise by doing a thing merely because others do it, no more than by believing a thing only because others believe it. If the grounds of an opinion are not conclusive to the person's own reason, his reason cannot be strengthened, but is likely to be weakened, by his adopting it: and if the inducements to an act are not such as are consentaneous to his own feelings and character (where affection, or the rights of others, are not concerned) it is so much done towards rendering his feelings and character inert and torpid, instead of active and energetic.

He who lets the world, or his own portion of it, choose his plan of life for him, has no need of any other faculty than the ape-like one of imitation. He who chooses his plan for himself, employs all his faculties. He must use observation to see, reasoning and judgment to foresee, activity to gather materials for decision, discrimination to decide, and when he has decided, firmness and self-control to hold to his deliberate decision. And these qualities he requires and exercises exactly in proportion as the part of his conduct which he determines according to his own judgment and feelings is a large one. It is possible that he might be guided in some good path, and kept out of harm's way, without any of these things. But what will be his comparative worth as a human being? It really is of importance, not only what men do, but also what manner of men they are that do it. Among the works of man, which human life is rightly employed in perfecting and beautifying, the first in importance surely is man himself. Supposing it were possible to get houses built, corn grown, battles fought, causes tried, and even churches erected and prayers said, by machinery—by automatons in human form—it would be a considerable loss to exchange for these automatons even the men and women who at present inhabit the more civilized parts of the world, and who assuredly are but starved specimens of what nature can and will produce. Human nature is not a machine to be built after a model, and set to do exactly the work prescribed for it, but a tree, which requires to grow and develope itself on all sides, according to the tendency of the inward forces which make it a living thing.

It will probably be conceded that it is desirable people should exercise their understandings, and that an intelligent following of custom, or even occasionally an intelligent deviation from custom, is better than a blind and simply mechanical adhesion to it. To a certain extent it is admitted, that our understanding should be our own: but there is not the same willingness to admit that our desires and impulses should be our own likewise: or that to possess impulses of our own, and of any strength, is anything but a peril and a snare. Yet desires and impulses are as much a part of a perfect human being, as beliefs and restraints: and strong impulses are only perilous when not properly balanced; when one set of aims and inclinations is developed into strength, while others, which ought to co-exist with them, remain weak and inactive. It is not because men's desires are strong that they act ill; it is because their consciences are weak. There is no natural connexion between strong impulses and a weak conscience. The natural connexion is the other way. To say that one person's desires and feelings are stronger and more various than those of another, is merely to say that he has more of the raw material of human nature, and is therefore capable, perhaps of more evil, but certainly of more good. Strong impulses are but another name for energy. Energy may be turned to bad uses; but more good may always be made of an energetic nature, than of an indolent and impassive one. Those who have most natural feeling, are always those whose cultivated feelings may be made the strongest. The same strong susceptibilities which make the personal impulses vivid and powerful, are also the source from whence are generated the most passionate love of virtue, and the sternest self-control. It is through the cultivation of these, that society both does its duty and protects its interests: not by rejecting the stuff of which heroes are made, because it knows not how to make them. A person whose desires and impulses are his own—are the expression of his own nature, as it has been developed and modified by his own culture—is said to have a character. One whose desires and impulses are not his own, has no character, no more than a steam-engine has a character. If, in addition to being his own, his impulses are strong, and are under the government of a strong will, he has an energetic character. Whoever thinks that individuality of desires and impulses should not be encouraged to unfold itself, must maintain that society has no need of strong natures—is not the better for containing many persons who have much character—and that a high general average of energy is not desirable.

In some early states of society, these forces might be, and were, too much ahead of the power which society then possessed of disciplining and controlling them. There has been a time when the element of spontaneity and individuality was in excess, and the social principle had a hard struggle with it. The difficulty then was, to induce men of strong bodies or minds to pay obedience to any rules which required them to control their impulses. To overcome this difficulty, law and discipline, like the Popes struggling against the Emperors, asserted a power over the whole man, claiming to control all his life in order to control his character—which society had not found any other sufficient means of binding. But society has now fairly got the better of individuality; and the danger which threatens human nature is not the excess, but the deficiency, of personal impulses and preferences. Things are vastly changed, since the passions of those who were strong by station or by personal endowment were in a state of habitual rebellion against laws and ordinances, and required to be rigorously chained up to enable the persons within their reach to enjoy any particle of security. In our times, from the highest class of society down to the lowest, every one lives as under the eye of a hostile and dreaded censorship. Not only in what concerns others, but in what concerns only themselves, the individual or the family do not ask themselves—what do I prefer? or, what would suit my character and disposition? or, what would allow the best and highest in me to have fair play, and enable it to grow and thrive? They ask themselves, what is suitable to my position? what is usually done by persons of my station and pecuniary circumstances? or (worse still) what is usually done by persons of a station and circumstances superior to mine? I do not mean that they choose what is customary, in preference to what suits their own inclination.

It does not occur to them to have any inclination, except for what is customary. Thus the mind itself is bowed to the yoke: even in what people do for pleasure, conformity is the first thing thought of; they like in crowds; they exercise choice only among things commonly done: peculiarity of taste, eccentricity of conduct, are shunned equally with crimes: until by dint of not following their own nature, they have no nature to follow: their human capacities are withered and starved: they become incapable of any strong wishes or native pleasures, and are generally without either opinions or feelings of home growth, or properly their own. Now is this, or is it not, the desirable condition of human nature?

It is so, on the Calvinistic theory. According to that, the one great offence of man is Self-will. All the good of which humanity is capable, is comprised in Obedience. You have no choice; thus you must do, and no otherwise: "whatever is not a duty, is a sin." Human nature being radically corrupt, there is no redemption for any one until human nature is killed within him. To one holding this theory of life, crushing out any of the human faculties, capacities, and susceptibilities, is no evil: man needs no capacity, but that of surrendering himself to the will of God: and if he uses any of his faculties for any other purpose but to do that supposed will more effectually, he is better without them. That is the theory of Calvinism; and it is held, in a mitigated form, by many who do not consider themselves Calvinists; the mitigation consisting in giving a less ascetic interpretation to the alleged will of God; asserting it to be his will that mankind should gratify some of their inclinations; of course not in the manner they themselves prefer, but in the way of obedience, that is, in a way prescribed to them by authority; and, therefore, by the necessary conditions of the case, the same for all.

In some such insidious form there is at present a strong tendency to this narrow theory of life, and to the pinched and hidebound type of human character which it patronizes. Many persons, no doubt, sincerely think that human beings thus cramped and dwarfed, are as their Maker designed them to be; just as many have thought that trees are a much finer thing when clipped into pollards, or cut out into figures of animals, than as nature made them. But if it be any part of religion to believe that man was made by a good Being, it is more consistent with that faith to believe, that this Being gave all human faculties that they might be cultivated and unfolded, not rooted out and consumed, and that he takes delight in every nearer approach made by his creatures to the ideal conception embodied in them, every increase in any of their capabilities of comprehension, of action, or of enjoyment. There is a different type of human excellence from the Calvinistic; a conception of humanity as having its nature bestowed on it for other purposes than merely to be abnegated. "Pagan self-assertion" is one of the elements of human worth, as well as "Christian self-denial." There is a Greek ideal of self-development, which the Platonic and Christian ideal of self-government blends with, but does not supersede. It may be better to be a John Knox than an Alcibiades, but it is better to be a Pericles than either; nor would a Pericles, if we had one in these days, be without anything good which belonged to John Knox.

It is not by wearing down into uniformity all that is individual in themselves, but by cultivating it and calling it forth, within the limits imposed by the rights and interests of others, that human beings become a noble and beautiful object of contemplation; and as the works partake the character of those who do them, by the same process human life also becomes rich, diversified, and animating, furnishing more abundant aliment to high thoughts and elevating feelings, and strengthening the tie which binds every individual to the race, by making the race infinitely better worth belonging to. In proportion to the development of his individuality, each person becomes more valuable to himself, and is therefore capable of being more valuable to others. There is a greater fulness of life about his own existence, and when there is more life in the units there is more in the mass which is composed of them. As much compression as is necessary to prevent the stronger specimens of human nature from encroaching on the rights of others, cannot be dispensed with; but for this there is ample compensation even in the point of view of human development. The means of development which the individual loses by being prevented from gratifying his inclinations to the injury of others, are chiefly obtained at the expense of the development of other people. And even to himself there is a full equivalent in the better development of the social part of his nature, rendered possible by the restraint put upon the selfish part. To be held to rigid rules of justice for the sake of others, developes the feelings and capacities which have the good of others for their object. But to be restrained in things not affecting their good, by their mere displeasure, developes nothing valuable, except such force of character as may unfold itself in resisting the restraint. If acquiesced in, it dulls and blunts the whole nature. To give any fair play to the nature of each, it is essential that different persons should be allowed to lead different lives. In proportion as this latitude has been exercised in any age, has that age been noteworthy to posterity. Even despotism does not produce its worst effects, so long as Individuality exists under it; and whatever crushes individuality is despotism, by whatever name it may be called, and whether it professes to be enforcing the will of God or the injunctions of men.

Having said that Individuality is the same thing with development, and that it is only the cultivation of individuality which produces, or can produce, well-developed human beings, I might here close the argument: for what more or better can be said of any condition of human affairs, than that it brings human beings themselves nearer to the best thing they can be? or what worse can be said of any obstruction to good, than that it prevents this? Doubtless, however, these considerations will not suffice to convince those who most need convincing; and it is necessary further to show, that these developed human beings are of some use to the undeveloped—to point out to those who do not desire liberty, and would not avail themselves of it, that they may be in some intelligible manner rewarded for allowing other people to make use of it without hindrance.

In the first place, then, I would suggest that they might possibly learn something from them. It will not be denied by anybody, that originality is a valuable element in human affairs. There is always need of persons not only to discover new truths, and point out when what were once truths are true no longer, but also to commence new practices, and set the example of more enlightened conduct, and better taste and sense in human life. This cannot well be gainsaid by anybody who does not believe that the world has already attained perfection in all its ways and practices. It is true that this benefit is not capable of being rendered by everybody alike: there are but few persons, in comparison with the whole of mankind, whose experiments, if adopted by others, would be likely to be any improvement on established practice. But these few are the salt of the earth; without them, human life would become a stagnant pool. Not only is it they who introduce good things which did not before exist; it is they who keep the life in those which already existed. If there were nothing new to be done, would human intellect cease to be necessary? Would it be a reason why those who do the old things should forget why they are done, and do them like cattle, not like human beings? There is only too great a tendency in the best beliefs and practices to degenerate into the mechanical; and unless there were a succession of persons whose ever-recurring originality prevents the grounds of those beliefs and practices from becoming merely traditional, such dead matter would not resist the smallest shock from anything really alive, and there would be no reason why civilization should not die out, as in the Byzantine Empire. Persons of genius, it is true, are, and are always likely to be, a small minority; but in order to have them, it is necessary to preserve the soil in which they grow. Genius can only breathe freely in an *atmosphere* of freedom. Persons of genius are, *ex vi termini,* more individual than any other people—less capable, consequently, of fitting themselves, without hurtful compression, into any of the small number of moulds which society provides in order to save its members the trouble of forming their own character. If from timidity they consent to be forced into one of these moulds, and to let all that part of themselves which cannot expand under the pressure remain unexpanded, society will be little the better for their genius. If they are of a strong character, and break their fetters, they become a mark for the society which has not succeeded in reducing them to commonplace, to point at with solemn warning as "wild," "erratic," and the like; much as if one should complain of the Niagara river for not flowing smoothly between its banks like a Dutch canal.

I insist thus emphatically on the importance of genius, and the necessity of allowing it to unfold itself freely both in thought and in practice, being well aware that no one will deny the position in theory, but knowing also that almost every one, in reality, is totally indifferent to it. People think genius a fine thing if it enables a man to write an exciting poem, or paint a picture. But in its true sense, that of originality in thought and action, though no one says that it is not a thing to be admired, nearly all, at heart, think that they can do very well without it. Unhappily this is too natural to be wondered at. Originality is the one thing which unoriginal minds cannot feel the use of. They cannot see what it is to do for them: how should they? If they could see what it would do for them, it would not be originality. The first service which originality has to render them, is that of opening their eyes: which being once fully done, they would have a chance of being themselves original. Meanwhile, recollecting that nothing was ever yet done which some one was not the first to do, and that all good things which exist are the fruits of originality, let them be modest enough to believe that there is something still left for it to accomplish, and assure themselves that they are more in need of originality, the less they are conscious of the want.

In sober truth, whatever homage may be professed, or even paid, to real or supposed mental superiority, the general tendency of things throughout the world is to render mediocrity the ascendant power among mankind. In ancient history, in the Middle Ages, and in a diminishing degree through the long transition from feudality to the present time, the individual was a power in himself; and if he had either great talents or a high social position, he was a considerable power. At present individuals are lost in the crowd. In politics it is almost a triviality to say that public opinion now rules the world. The only power deserving the name is that of masses, and of governments while they make themselves the organ of the tendencies and instincts of masses. This is as true in the moral and social relations of private life as in public transactions. Those whose opinions go by the name of public opinion, are not always the same sort of public: in

America they are the whole white population; in England, chiefly the middle class. But they are always a mass, that is to say, collective mediocrity. And what is a still greater novelty, the mass do not now take their opinions from dignitaries in Church or State, from ostensible leaders, or from books. Their thinking is done for them by men much like themselves, addressing them or speaking in their name, on the spur of the moment, through the newspapers. I am not complaining of all this. I do not assert that anything better is compatible, as a general rule, with the present low state of the human mind. But that does not hinder the government of mediocrity from being mediocre government. No government by a democracy or a numerous aristocracy, either in its political acts or in the opinions, qualities, and tone of mind which it fosters, ever did or could rise above mediocrity, except in so far as the sovereign Many have let themselves be guided (which in their best times they always have done) by the counsels and influence of a more highly gifted and instructed One or Few. The initiation of all wise or noble things, comes and must come from individuals; generally at first from some one individual. The honour and glory of the average man is that he is capable of following that initiative; that he can respond internally to wise and noble things, and be led to them with his eyes open. I am not countenancing the sort of "hero-worship" which applauds the strong man of genius for forcibly seizing on the government of the world and making it do his bidding in spite of itself. All he can claim is, freedom to point out the way. The power of compelling others into it, is not only inconsistent with the freedom and development of all the rest, but corrupting to the strong man himself. It does seem, however, that when the opinions of masses of merely average men are everywhere become or becoming the dominant power, the counterpoise and corrective to that tendency would be, the more and more pronounced individuality of those who stand on the higher eminences of thought. It is in these circumstances most especially, that exceptional individuals, instead of being deterred, should be encouraged in acting differently from the mass. In other times there was no advantage in their doing so, unless they acted not only differently, but better. In this age, the mere example of nonconformity, the mere refusal to bend the knee to custom, is itself a service. Precisely because the tyranny of opinion is such as to make eccentricity a reproach, it is desirable, in order to break through that tyranny, that people should be eccentric. Eccentricity has always abounded when and where strength of character has abounded; and the amount of eccentricity in a society has generally been proportional to the amount of genius, mental vigor, and moral courage which it contained. That so few now dare to be eccentric, marks the chief danger of the time.

I have said that it is important to give the freest scope possible to uncustomary things, in order that it may in time appear which of these are fit to be converted into customs. But independence of action, and disregard of custom, are not solely deserving of encouragement for the chance they afford that better modes of action, and customs more worthy of general adoption, may be struck out; nor is it only persons of decided mental superiority who have a just claim to carry on their lives in their own way. There is no reason that all human existence should be constructed on some one or some small number of patterns. If a person possesses any tolerable amount of common sense and experience, his own mode of laying out his existence is the best, not because it is the best in itself, but because it is his own mode. Human beings are not like sheep; and even sheep are not undistinguishably alike. A man cannot get a coat or a pair of boots to fit him, unless they are either made to his measure, or he has a whole warehouseful to choose from: and is it easier to fit him with a life than with a coat, or are human beings more like one another in their whole physical and spiritual conformation than in the shape of their feet? If it were only that people have diversities of taste, that is reason enough for not attempting to shape them all after one model. But different persons also require different conditions for their spiritual development; and can no more exist healthily in the same moral, than all the variety of plants can in the same physical, atmosphere and climate. The same things which are helps to one person towards the cultivation of his higher nature, are hindrances to another. The same mode of life is a healthy excitement to one, keeping all his faculties of action and enjoyment in their best order, while to another it is a distracting burthen, which suspends or crushes all internal life. Such are the differences among human beings in their sources of pleasure, their susceptibilities of pain, and the operation on them of different physical and moral agencies, that unless there is a corresponding diversity in their modes of life, they neither obtain their fair share of happiness, nor grow up to the mental, moral, and aesthetic stature of which their nature is capable. Why then should tolerance, as far as the public sentiment is concerned, extend only to tastes and modes of life which extort acquiescence by the multitude of their adherents? Nowhere (except in some monastic institutions) is diversity of taste entirely unrecognized; a person may, without blame, either like or dislike rowing, or smoking, or music, or athletic exercises, or chess, or cards, or study, because both those who like each of these things, and those who dislike them, are too numerous to be put down. But the man, and still more the woman, who can be accused either of doing "what nobody does," or of not doing "what everybody does," is the subject of as much depreciatory remark as if he or she had committed some grave moral delinquency. Persons require to possess a title, or some other badge of rank, or of the consideration of people of rank, to be able to indulge somewhat in the luxury of doing as they like without detriment to their estimation. To indulge somewhat, I repeat: for whoever allow themselves much of that indulgence, incur the risk of something worse than disparaging speeches—they are in peril of a commission *de lunatico*, and of having their property taken from them and given to their relations.

There is one characteristic of the present direction of public opinion, peculiarly calculated to make it intolerant of any marked demonstration of individuality. The general average of mankind are not only moderate in intellect, but also moderate in inclinations: they have no tastes or wishes strong enough to incline them to do anything unusual, and they consequently do not understand those who have, and class all such with the wild and intemperate whom they are accustomed to look down upon. Now, in addition to this fact which is general, we have only to suppose that a strong movement has set in towards the improvement of morals, and it is evident what we have to expect. In these days such a movement has set in; much has actually been effected in the way of increased regularity of conduct, and discouragement of excesses; and there is a philanthropic spirit abroad, for the exercise of which there is no more inviting field than the moral and prudential improvement of our fellow-creatures. These tendencies of the times cause the public to be more disposed than at most former periods to prescribe general rules of conduct, and endeavor to make every one conform to the approved standard. And that standard, express or tacit, is to desire nothing strongly. Its ideal of character is to be without any marked character; to maim by compression, like a Chinese lady's foot, every part of human nature which stands out prominently, and tends to make the person markedly dissimilar in outline to commonplace humanity.

As is usually the case with ideals which exclude one-half of what is desirable, the present standard of approbation produces only an inferior imitation of the other half. Instead of great energies guided by vigorous reason, and strong feelings strongly controlled by a conscientious will, its result is weak feelings and weak energies, which therefore can be kept in outward conformity to rule without any strength either of will or of reason. Already energetic characters on any large scale are becoming merely traditional. There is now scarcely any outlet for energy in this country except business. The energy expended in that may still be regarded as considerable. What little is left from that employment, is expended on some hobby; which may be a useful, even a philanthropic hobby, but is always some one thing, and generally a thing of small dimensions. The greatness of England is now all collective: individually small, we only appear capable of anything great by our habit of combining; and with this our moral and religious philanthropists are perfectly contented. But it was men of another stamp than this that made England what it has been; and men of another stamp will be needed to prevent its decline.

The despotism of custom is everywhere the standing hindrance to human advancement, being in unceasing antagonism to that disposition to aim at something better than customary, which is called, according to circumstances, the spirit of liberty, or that of progress or improvement. The spirit of improvement is not always a spirit of liberty, for it may aim at forcing improvements on an unwilling people; and the spirit of liberty, in so far as it resists such attempts, may ally itself locally and temporarily with the opponents of improvement; but the only unfailing and permanent source of improvement is liberty, since by it there are as many possible independent centres of improvement as there are individuals. The progressive principle, however, in either shape, whether as the love of liberty or of improvement, is antagonistic to the sway of Custom, involving at least emancipation from that yoke; and the contest between the two constitutes the chief interest of the history of mankind. The greater part of the world has, properly speaking, no history, because the despotism of Custom is complete. This is the case over the whole East. Custom is there, in all things, the final appeal; justice and right mean conformity to custom; the argument of custom no one, unless some tyrant intoxicated with power, thinks of resisting. And we see the result. Those nations must once have had originality; they did not start out of the ground populous, lettered, and versed in many of the arts of life; they made themselves all this, and were then the greatest and most powerful nations in the world. What are they now? The subjects or dependents of tribes whose forefathers wandered in the forests when theirs had magnificent palaces and gorgeous temples, but over whom custom exercised only a divided rule with liberty and progress. A people, it appears, may be progressive for a certain length of time, and then stop: when does it stop? When it ceases to possess individuality. If a similar change should befall the nations of Europe, it will not be in exactly the same shape: the despotism of custom with which these nations are threatened is not precisely stationariness. It proscribes singularity, but it does not preclude change, provided all change together. We have discarded the fixed costumes of our forefathers; every one must still dress like other people, but the fashion may change once or twice a year. We thus take care that when there is change it shall be for change's sake, and not from any idea of beauty or convenience; for the same idea of beauty or convenience would not strike all the world at the same moment, and be simultaneously thrown aside by all at another moment. But we are progressive as well as changeable: we continually make new inventions in mechanical things, and keep them until they are again superseded by better; we are eager for improvement in politics, in education, even in morals, though in this last our idea of improvement chiefly consists in persuading or forcing other people to be as good as ourselves. It is not progress that we object to; on the contrary, we flatter ourselves that we are the most progressive people who ever lived. It is individuality that we war against: we should think we had done wonders if we had made ourselves all alike; forgetting that the unlikeness of one person to another is generally the first thing which draws the attention of either to the imperfection of his own type, and the superiority of another, or the possibility, by combining the advantages of both, of producing something better than either. We have a warning example in China—a nation of much talent, and, in some respects, even wisdom, owing to the rare good fortune of having been provided at an early period with a particularly good set of customs, the work, in some measure, of men to whom even the most enlightened European must accord, under certain limitations, the title of sages and philosophers. They are remarkable, too, in the excellence of their apparatus for impressing, as far as possible, the best wisdom they possess upon every mind in the community, and securing that those who have appropriated most of it shall occupy the posts of honour and power. Surely the people who did this have discovered the secret of human progressiveness, and must have kept themselves steadily at the head of the movement of the world. On the contrary, they have become stationary—have remained so for thousands of years; and if they are ever to be farther improved, it must be by foreigners. They have succeeded beyond all hope in what English philanthropists are so industriously working at—in making a people all alike, all governing their thoughts and conduct by the same maxims and rules; and these are the fruits. The modern regime of public opinion is, in an unorganized form, what the Chinese educational and political systems are in an organized; and unless individuality shall be able successfully to assert itself against this yoke, Europe, notwithstanding its noble antecedents and its professed Christianity, will tend to become another China.

What is it that has hitherto preserved Europe from this lot? What has made the European family of nations an improving, instead of a stationary portion of mankind? Not any superior excellence in them, which, when it exists, exists as the effect, not as the cause; but their remarkable diversity of character and culture. Individuals, classes, nations, have been extremely unlike one another: they have struck out a great variety of paths, each leading to something valuable; and although at every period those who travelled in different paths have been intolerant of one another, and each would have thought it an excellent thing if all the rest could have been compelled to travel his road, their attempts to thwart each other's development have rarely had any permanent success, and each has in time endured to receive the good which the others have offered. Europe is, in my judgment, wholly indebted to this plurality of paths for its progressive and many-sided development. But it already begins to possess this benefit in a considerably less degree. It is decidedly advancing towards the Chinese ideal of making all people alike. M. de Tocqueville, in his last important work, remarks how much more the Frenchmen of the present day resemble one another, than did those even of the last generation. The same remark might be made of Englishmen in a far greater degree. In a passage already quoted from Wilhelm Von Humboldt, he points out two things as necessary conditions of human development, because necessary to render people unlike one another; namely, freedom, and variety of situations. The second of these two conditions is in this country every day diminishing. The circumstances which surround different classes and individuals, and shape their characters, are daily becoming more assimilated. Formerly, different ranks, different neighbourhoods, different trades and professions, lived in what might be called different worlds; at present, to a great degree in the same. Comparatively speaking, they now read the same things, listen to the same things, see the same things, go to the same places, have their hopes and fears directed to the same objects, have the same rights and liberties, and the same means of asserting them. Great as are the differences of position which remain, they are nothing to those which have ceased. And the assimilation is still proceeding. All the political changes of the age promote it, since they all tend to raise the low and to lower the high. Every extension of education promotes it, because education brings people under common influences, and gives them access to the general stock of facts and sentiments. Improvements in the means of communication promote it, by bringing the inhabitants of distant places into personal contact, and keeping up a rapid flow of changes of residence between one place and another. The increase of commerce and manufactures promotes it, by diffusing more widely the advantages of easy circumstances, and opening all objects of ambition, even the highest, to general competition, whereby the desire of rising becomes no longer the character of a particular class, but of all classes. A more powerful agency than even all these, in bringing about a general similarity among mankind, is the complete establishment, in this and other free countries, of the ascendancy of public opinion in the State. As the various social eminences which enabled persons entrenched on them to disregard the opinion of the multitude, gradually become levelled; as the very idea of resisting the will of the public, when it is positively known that they have a will, disappears more and more from the minds of practical politicians; there ceases to be any social support for nonconformity—any substantive power in society, which, itself opposed to the ascendancy of numbers, is interested in taking under its protection opinions and tendencies at variance with those of the public.

The combination of all these causes forms so great a mass of influences hostile to Individuality, that it is not easy to see how it can stand its ground. It will do so with increasing difficulty, unless the intelligent part of the public can be made to feel its value— to see that it is good there should be differences, even though not for the better, even though, as it may appear to them, some should be for the worse. If the claims of Individuality are ever to be asserted, the time is now, while much is still wanting to complete the enforced assimilation. It is only in the earlier stages that any stand can be successfully made against the encroachment. The demand that all other people shall resemble ourselves, grows by what it feeds on. If resistance waits till life is reduced nearly to one uniform type, all deviations from that type will come to be considered impious, immoral, even monstrous and contrary to nature. Mankind speedily become unable to conceive diversity, when they have been for some time unaccustomed to see it.

3. FROM *THE SOUL OF MAN UNDER SOCIALISM*

OSCAR WILDE

Originally published in *The Fortnightly Review,* February 1891

Oscar Fingal O'Flahertie Wilde (1854–1900) was an Irish essayist, playwright, novelist, and intellectual in Victorian England. In 1895, Wilde was convicted of "gross indecency"—a result of his love affair with Lord Alfred "Bosie" Douglas—and was sentenced to two years of hard labor. In the passage excerpted here from The Soul of Man Under Socialism, *Wilde argues in stirring prose that individualism is inherent in human nature and should be cultivated to its highest level. Individualism, according to Wilde, is the only foundation on which a true and lasting sympathy for others can be built.*

It is to be noted also that Individualism does not come to man with any sickly cant about duty, which merely means doing what other people want because they want it; or any hideous cant about self-sacrifice, which is merely a survival of savage mutilation. In fact, it does not come to man with any claims upon him at all. It comes naturally and inevitably out of man. It is the point to which all development tends. It is the differentiation to which all organisms grow. It is the perfection that is inherent in every mode of life, and towards which every mode of life quickens. And so Individualism exercises no compulsion over man. On the contrary, it says to man that he should suffer no compulsion to be exercised over him. It does not try to force people to be good. It knows that people are good when they are let alone. Man will develop Individualism out of himself. Man is now so developing Individualism. To ask whether Individualism is practical is like asking whether Evolution is practical. Evolution is the law of life, and there is no evolution except towards Individualism. Where this tendency is not expressed, it is a case of artificially-arrested growth, or of disease, or of death.

Individualism will also be unselfish and unaffected. It has been pointed out that one of the results of the extraordinary tyranny of authority is that words are absolutely distorted from their proper and simple meaning, and are used to express the obverse of their right signification. What is true about Art is true about Life. A man is called affected, nowadays, if he dresses as he likes to dress. But in doing that he is acting in a perfectly natural manner. Affectation, in such matters, consists in dressing according to the views of one's neighbour, whose views, as they are the views of the majority, will probably be extremely stupid. Or a man is called selfish if he lives in the manner that seems to him most suitable for the full realisation of his own personality; if, in fact, the primary aim of his life is self-development. But this is the way in which everyone should live. Selfishness is not living as one wishes to live, it is asking others to live as one wishes to live. And unselfishness is letting other people's lives alone, not interfering with them. Selfishness always aims at creating around it an absolute uniformity of type. Unselfishness recognises infinite variety of type as a delightful thing, accepts it, acquiesces in it, enjoys it. It is not selfish to think for oneself. A man who does not think for himself does not think at all. It is grossly selfish to require of one's neighbour that he should think in the same way, and hold the same opinions. Why should he? If he can think, he will probably think differently. If he cannot think, it is monstrous to require thought of any kind from him. A red rose is not selfish because it wants to be a red rose. It would be horribly selfish if it wanted all the other flowers in the garden to be both red and roses. Under Individualism people will be quite natural and absolutely unselfish, and will know the meanings of the words, and realise them in their free, beautiful lives. Nor will men be egotistic as they are now. For the egotist is he who makes claims upon others, and the Individualist will not desire to do that. It will not give him pleasure. When man has realised Individualism, he will also realise sympathy and exercise it freely and spontaneously. Up to the present man has hardly cultivated sympathy at all. He has merely sympathy with pain, and sympathy with pain is not the highest form of sympathy. All sympathy is fine, but sympathy with suffering is the least fine mode. It is tainted with egotism. It is apt to become morbid. There is in it a certain element of terror for our own safety. We become afraid that we ourselves might be as the leper or as the blind, and that no man would have care of us. It is curiously limiting, too. One should sympathise with the entirety of life, not with life's sores and maladies merely, but with life's joy and beauty and energy and health and freedom. The wider sympathy is, of course, the more difficult. It requires more unselfishness. Anybody can sympathise with the sufferings of a friend, but it requires a very fine nature—it requires, in fact, the nature of a true Individualist—to sympathise with a friend's success.

4. "OF PREPARATION"

MICHEL DE MONTAIGNE

The Essays of Montaigne, trans. E. J. Trechmann (New York: Oxford University Press, 1927)

Michel de Montaigne (1533–92) was a French nobleman and states-man who retreated to private life during the French Wars of Religion. Montaigne is credited with refining the literary form of the essay, with its emphasis on self-reflection and individualism. His essays depict a man with profound psychological insight and a liberal temperament. Montaigne published The Essays *in three volumes between 1580 and 1588. In the passage excerpted here, Montaigne discusses the importance of knowing oneself.*

For many years now my thoughts have had no other aim but myself, I have studied and examined myself only, and if I study any other things, it is to apply them immediately to, or rather within, myself. And I do not think I go wrong if, as is done in other incomparably less profitable sciences, I communicate what I have learned in this one, although I am not very well satisfied with the progress I have made therein. There is no description equal in difficulty to a description of oneself, and certainly none in profitableness. Besides, a man must curl his hair, he must trim and pull himself together, to appear in public. Now I am contin-ually doing myself up, for I am continually describing myself.

Custom has made it a fault to speak of oneself, and obstinately forbids it, in hatred of the boasting which always seems to attach to self-testimony. Instead of wiping a child's nose, that is called cutting it off.

> How often we, in eagerness to shun
> One fault, are apt into a worse to run. (HORACE.)

To me there seems to be more harm than good in this remedy. But, though it were true that to talk to people about ourselves is necessarily a presumption, I must not, whilst pursuing my general plan, forbear an action which makes public this morbid peculiarity, since it is in me. I ought not to conceal this fault which I not only practise but profess. At all events, to speak my mind freely, it is the same wrong opinion that condemns wine because some get drunk with it. Only the things that are good can be abused. And I believe that this rule only concerns the popular failing. Such rules are bridles for calves, with which neither saints who speak so highly of themselves, nor philosophers, nor theologians will curb themselves. Nor will I, though I am as little the one as the other. If they do not expressly write about themselves, at all events, when the occasion arises, they do not hesitate to push themselves forward into the highest seats.

Of what does Socrates treat more largely than himself? What does he make his disciples talk about more often than themselves—not the lessons of their book, but the essence and motions of their soul?

We devoutly confess to God and our confessor, as our neighbours do to the whole people. 'But, I may be answered, we confess only our sins'. Then we confess all, for our very virtue is faulty and repentable. My trade and art is to live. He who forbids me to speak of it according to my understanding, experience, and habit, may as well expect an architect to speak of buildings, not as he himself regards them, but as his neighbour does, not from his own knowledge, but from another's. If it is vainglory for a man spontaneously to cry out his own virtues, why does not Cicero commend the eloquence of Hortensius, and Hortensius that of Cicero?

Perhaps they would rather I gave testimony of myself by words and deeds, not merely by words. I chiefly paint my thoughts: a shapeless subject, and incapable of being translated into acts. It is all I can do to couch it in this airy body of the voice. Wiser men and more devout have lived and avoided all conspicuous actions. My actions would be rather the result of chance than a reflection of my soul. They testify to the part they play, not to the part I play, unless it be conjecturally and uncertainly: samples which show off only the details. I exhibit myself entire: it is a skeleton on which, at one view, appear the veins, the muscles, and the tendons, each in its own place. One part is brought into evidence by a cough, another by pallor or palpitation of the heart, and that dubiously. It is not my deeds that I write of; it is myself, it is my essence.

I am of opinion that we should be cautious in forming an estimate of ourselves, and equally conscientious in expressing it impartially, whether it be high or low. If I thought myself good or wise, or nearly so, I should shout it at the top of my voice. To make ourselves out worse than we are is foolishness, not modesty. To be content with less than we are worth is want of spirit and pusillanimity, according to Aristotle. No virtue is helped by falsehood, and the truth is never subject to error. To declare ourselves better than we are is not always presumption, it too is often foolishness. To be inordinately pleased with oneself, to be inconsiderately in love with oneself, is, in my opinion, the substance of this error. The supreme remedy for curing it is to do the very opposite of what they enjoin who, by forbidding us to speak of ourselves, consequently still more forbid us to think of ourselves. Pride lies in thought; the tongue can have only a very small share in it.

They imagine that to muse on oneself is to be pleased with oneself, that to associate and converse with oneself is to hold oneself too dear. That may be. But this excess is only bred in those who touch only on their surface, who view themselves according to their circumstances, who call it dreaming and idleness to commune with themselves, and regard the building up and furnishing of one's mind as a mere building of castles in Spain; looking upon themselves as a third person and a stranger.

If any man, looking down on those beneath him, is intoxicated with his own knowledge, let him turn his eyes upwards to the past ages, and he will lower his horns; for there he will find so many thousands of minds that will tread him under foot. If he entertain any flattering conceit of his own worth, let him remember the lives of the two Scipios, and the many armies and nations that leave him so far behind them. No particular virtue will put pride into the heart of him who will at the same time take account of the many other feeble and imperfect qualities that are in him, ending up with the nothingness of man's estate.

Because Socrates alone had honestly bitten into that precept of his God, 'Know thyself', and had by that study come to despise himself, he alone was thought to deserve the title of Sage. Whoever shall so know himself, let him boldly make himself known by his own mouth.

PART TWO

SOCIAL INDIVIDUALISM

5. FROM "WHAT IS AN AMERICAN?"

J. HECTOR ST. JOHN DE CRÈVECOEUR

Letters from an American Farmer (New York: Duffield and Co., 1908)

J. Hector St. John de Crèvecoeur (1735–1813) served as a surveyor with the French army during the French and Indian War (1754–63). After the war was over, Crèvecoeur purchased a farm in New York and prospered. The following excerpt is from the third of Crèvecoeur's Letters from an American Farmer, *first published in 1782. It is a classic statement of American individualism.*

I wish I could be acquainted with the feelings and thoughts which must agitate the heart and present themselves to the mind of an enlightened Englishman, when he first lands on this continent. . . .

. . . He is arrived on a new continent; a modern society offers itself to his contemplation, different from what he had hitherto seen. It is not composed, as in Europe, of great lords who possess every thing, and of a herd of people who have nothing. Here are no aristocratical families, no courts, no kings, no bishops, no ecclesiastical dominion, no invisible power giving to a few a very visible one; no great manufacturers employing thousands, no great refinements of luxury. The rich and the poor are not so far removed from each other as they are in Europe. Some few towns excepted, we are all tillers of the earth, from Nova Scotia to West Florida. We are a people of cultivators, scattered over an immense territory, communicating with each other by means of good roads and navigable rivers, united by the silken bands of mild government, all respecting the laws, without dreading their power, because they are equitable. We are all animated with the spirit of an industry which is unfettered and unrestrained, because each person works for himself. If he travels through our rural districts he views not the hostile castle, and the haughty mansion, contrasted with the clay-built hut and miserable cabin, where cattle and men help to keep each other warm, and dwell in meanness, smoke, and indigence. A pleasing uniformity of decent competence appears throughout our habitations. The meanest of our log-houses is a dry and comfortable habitation. Lawyer or merchant are the fairest titles our towns afford; that of a farmer is the only appellation of the rural inhabitants of our country. It must take some time ere he can reconcile himself to our dictionary, which is but short in words of dignity, and names of honour. There, on a Sunday, he sees a congregation of respectable farmers and their wives, all clad in neat homespun, well mounted, or riding in their own humble wagons. There is not among them an esquire, saving the unlettered magistrate. There he sees a parson as simple as his flock, a farmer who does not riot on the labour of others. We have no princes, for whom we toil, starve, and bleed: we are the most perfect society now existing in the world. Here man is free as he ought to be.

6. FROM *THE CITY OF GOD*

ST. AUGUSTINE OF HIPPO

Concerning the City of God Against the Pagans, trans. Curtis Tate (2014)

St. Augustine (354–428) was one of the most influential philosophers in the history of the Western world. This passage from his most famous book, The City of God, *is an early expression of the belief that individuals are the ultimate units of societies and states.*

I want to first inquire a little into that reason and sensibility which exists in wishing for the glory of empire on account of its girth and continuance when you cannot demonstrate felicity of the men who withered in the ruins of war wrapped in horror and bloody desire, always in blood foreign and domestic, yet still human. The result is a flickering joy akin to glass in its fragility, to which is attributed the terrible anxiety that it could suddenly shatter.

That this might more easily be adjudicated, let us not vanish beneath the fluid void of boasting and not blunt the sharp edge of our purpose when we hear lofty talk of "peoples," "kingdoms," and "provinces." Instead let us imagine two men; for a single man is like one word in a sermon, thus he is an element of a city or kingdom, whatever its scope in the occupation of spacious lands. Of the two men one is impoverished, even middle-class rather, and the other we shall think is extravagantly rich. The rich man is laden with terrors, melting under sorrow, emblazoned with aspirations; never is he secure, always he is restless and out of breath in the perpetual contentions of his enemies. Truly he makes a lot with the miseries of his inheritance, and yet with those profits he amasses caustic worries in his immense form. The poorer man is at ease with his family and what little he has. He is most dear to his own, he is delighted with the sweet peace of his friends, religious in his faith, mild mannered, of a healthy body, frugal in life, adherent to his traditions, and secure in his conscience. I do not think anyone so irrational that he would dare to doubt which man is preferable.

Therefore as it is with these two men, thus it is in two families, two peoples, and in two kingdoms. What with the basic principle of justice having been summoned correctly (if our purpose is set right), we will easily see where emptiness and happiness reside.

7. FROM *TWO DISCOURSES ON LIBERTY*

NATHANIEL NILES

Two Discourses on Liberty (1774). *American Political Writing during the Founding Era 1760–1805,* vol. 1, ed. Charles S. Hyneman and Donald S. Lutz (Indianapolis: Liberty Fund, 1983)

The American statesman Nathaniel Niles (1741–1828) was a graduate of Harvard and Princeton, where he studied law, medicine, and theology. Niles served Vermont in both the state and national legislatures. In the passage excerpted below from his political writings, Niles argues that social and political change begin with the individual.

Ages are composed of seconds, the earth of sands, and the sea of drops, too small to be seen by the naked eye. The smallest particles have their influence. Such is our state, that each individual has a proportion of influence on some neighbour at least; he, on another, and so on; as in a river, the following drop urges that which is before, and every one through the whole length of the stream has the like influence. We know not, what individuals may do. We are not at liberty to lie dormant until we can, at once, influence the whole. We must begin with the weight we have. Should the little springs neglect to flow till a general agreement should take place, the torrent that now bears down all before it, would never be formed. These mighty floods have their rise in single drops from the rocks, which, uniting, creep along till they meet with another combination so small that it might be absorbed by the traveller's foot. These unite, proceed, enlarge, till mountains tremble at their sound. Let us receive instruction from the streams, and without discouragement, pursue a laudable plan.

8. FROM "THE DOMINANT IDEA"

VOLTAIRINE DE CLEYRE

Selected Works of Voltairine de Cleyre, ed. Alexander Berkman (New York: Mother Earth Publishing Association, 1914)

The American freethinker and individualist–feminist Voltairine de Cleyre (1866–1912) was known in radical circles for her advocacy of "anarchism without adjectives." This phrase expressed de Cleyre's belief that any type of voluntary society is acceptable, so long as it embodies the voluntary cooperation of all members. In this excerpt from one of her most famous essays, de Cleyre explains the implications of committing oneself to the ideal of individual freedom.

It is not to be supposed that any one will attain to the full realization of what he purposes, even when those purposes do not involve united action with others; he *will* fall short; he will in some measure be overcome by contending or inert opposition. But something he will attain, if he continues to aim high.

What, then, would I have? you ask. I would have men invest themselves with the dignity of an aim higher than the chase for wealth; choose a thing to do in life outside of the making of things, and keep it in mind—not for a day, nor a year, but for a lifetime. And then keep faith with themselves! Not be a light-o'-love, to-day professing this and to-morrow that, and easily reading one self out of both whenever it becomes convenient; not advocating a thing to-day, and to-morrow kissing its enemies' sleeve, with that weak, coward cry in the mouth, "Circumstances make me." Take a good look into yourself, and if you love Things and the power and the plenitude of Things better than you love your own dignity, human dignity, Oh, say so, say so! Say it to yourself, and abide by it. But do not blow hot and cold in one breath. Do not try to be a social reformer and a respected possessor of Things at the same time. Do not preach the straight and narrow way while going joyously upon the wide one. *Preach the wide one,* or do not preach at all; but do not fool yourself by saying you would like to help usher in a free society, but you cannot sacrifice an armchair for it. Say honestly, "I love armchairs better than free men, and pursue them because I choose; not because circumstances make me. I love hats, large, large hats, with many feathers and great bows; and I would rather have those hats than trouble myself about social dreams that will never be accomplished in my day. The world worships hats, and I wish to worship with them."

But if you choose the liberty and pride and strength of the single soul, and the free fraternization of men, as the purpose which your life is to make manifest, then do not sell it for tinsel. Think that your soul is strong and will hold its way; and slowly, through bitter struggle perhaps, the strength will grow. And the foregoing of possessions for which others barter the last possibility of freedom, will become easy.

At the end of life you may close your eyes, saying: "I have not been dominated by the Dominant Idea of my Age; I have chosen mine own allegiance, and served it. I have proved by a lifetime that there is that in man which saves him from the absolute tyranny of Circumstance, which in the end conquers and re-moulds Circumstance,–the immortal fire of Individual Will, which is the salvation of the Future."

Let us have Men, Men who will say a word to their souls and keep it—keep it not when it is easy, but keep it when it is hard—keep it when the storm roars and there is a white-streaked sky and blue thunder before, and one's eyes are blinded and one's ears deafened with the war of opposing things; and keep it under the long leaden sky and the gray dreariness that never lifts. Hold unto the last: that is what it means to have a Dominant Idea.

9. FROM *A VINDICATION OF THE RIGHTS OF WOMAN*

MARY WOLLSTONECRAFT

A Vindication of the Rights of Woman (New York, A. J. Matsell, 1833)

Mary Wollstonecraft (1759–97) was one of the most remarkable and fiercely independent women of her time. She wished to liberate women from the constraints of traditional roles so that they could develop—through the use of reason—their individuality. Although Wollstonecraft expressed ideas that were regarded as radical during the 18th century, many of them have become integral to contemporary views about the importance of female independence. The following is the complete introduction to A Vindication of the Rights of Woman, *published in 1792.*

After considering the historic page, and viewing the living world with anxious solicitude, the most melancholy emotions of sorrowful indignation have depressed my spirits, and I have sighed when obliged to confess, that either nature has made a great difference between man and man, or that the civilization which has hitherto taken place in the world, has been very partial. I have turned over various books written on the subject of education, and patiently observed the conduct of parents and the management of schools; but what has been the result? a profound conviction, that the neglected education of my fellow creatures is the grand source of the misery I deplore; and that women in particular, are rendered weak and wretched by a variety of concurring causes, originating from one hasty conclusion. The conduct and manners of women, in fact evidently prove, that their minds are not in a healthy state; for, like the flowers that are planted in too rich a soil, strength and usefulness are sacrificed to beauty; and the flaunting leaves, after having pleased a fastidious eye, fade, disregarded on the stalk, long before the season when they ought to have arrived at maturity. One cause of this barren blooming I attribute to a false system of education, gathered from the books written on this subject by men, who, considering females rather as women than human creatures, have been more anxious to make them alluring mistresses than affectionate wives and rational mothers; and the understanding of the sex has been so bubbled by this specious homage, that the civilized women of the present century, with a few exceptions, are only anxious to inspire love, when they ought to cherish a nobler ambition, and by their abilities and virtues exact respect.

In a treatise, therefore, on female rights and manners, the works which have been particularly written for their improvement must not be overlooked; especially when it is asserted, in direct terms, that the minds of women are enfeebled by false refinement; that the books of instruction, by men of genius, have had the same tendency written as more frivolous productions; and that, in the true style of Mahometanism, they are only considered as females, and not as a part of the human species, when improvable reason is allowed to be the dignified distinction, which raises men above the brute creation, and puts a natural sceptre in a feeble hand.

Yet, because I am a woman, I would not lead my readers to suppose, that I mean violently to agitate the contested question respecting the equality and inferiority of the sex; but as the subject lies in my way, and I cannot pass it over without subjecting the main tendency of my reasoning to misconstruction, I shall stop a moment to deliver, in a few words, my opinion. In the government of the physical world, it is observable that the female, in general, is inferior to the male. The male pursues, the female yields—this is the law of nature; and it does not appear to be suspended or abrogated in favour of woman. This physical superiority cannot be denied—and it is a noble prerogative! But not content with this natural pre-eminence, men endeavour to sink us still lower, merely to render us alluring objects for a moment; and woman, intoxicated by the adoration which men, under the influence of their senses, pay them, do not seek to obtain a durable interest in their hearts, or to become the friends of the fellow creatures who find amusement in their society.

I am aware of an obvious inference: from every quarter have I heard exclamations against masculine women; but where are they to be found? If, by this appellation, men mean to inveigh against their ardour in hunting, shooting, and gaming, I shall most cordially join in the cry; but if it be, against the imitation of manly virtues, or, more properly speaking, the attainment of those talents and virtues, the exercise of which ennobles the human character, and which raise females in the scale of animal being, when they are comprehensively termed mankind—all those who view them with a philosophical eye must, I should think, wish with me, that they may every day grow more and more masculine.

This discussion naturally divides the subject. I shall first consider women in the grand light of human creatures, who, in common with men, are placed on this earth to unfold their faculties; and afterwards I shall more particularly point out their peculiar designation.

I wish also to steer clear of an error, which many respectable writers have fallen into; for the instruction which has hither been addressed to women, has rather been applicable to *ladies,* if the little indirect advice, that is scattered through Sandford and Merton, be excepted; but, addressing my sex in a firmer tone, I pay particular attention to those in the middle class, because they appear to be in the most natural state. Perhaps the seeds of false refinement, immorality, and vanity have ever been shed by the great. Weak, artificial beings raised above the common wants and affections of their race, in a premature unnatural manner, undermine the very foundation of virtue, and spread corruption through the whole mass of society! As a class of mankind they have the strongest claim to pity! The education of the rich tends to render them vain and helpless, and the unfolding mind is not strengthened by the practice of those duties which dignify the human character. They only live to amuse themselves, and by the same law which in nature invariably produces certain effects, they soon only afford barren amusement.

But as I purpose taking a separate view of the different ranks of society, and of the moral character of women, in each, this hint is, for the present, sufficient; and I have only alluded to the subject, because it appears to me to be the very essence of an introduction to give a cursory account of the contents of the work it introduces.

My own sex, I hope, will excuse me, if I treat them like rational creatures, instead of flattering their *fascinating* graces, and viewing them as if they were in a state of perpetual childhood, unable to stand alone. I earnestly wish to point out in what true dignity and human happiness consists—I wish to persuade women to endeavour to acquire strength, both of mind and body, and to convince them, that the soft phrases, susceptibility of heart, delicacy of sentiment, and refinement of taste, are almost synonymous with epithets of weakness, and that those beings who are only the objects of pity and that kind of love, which has been termed its sister, will soon become objects of contempt.

Dismissing then those pretty feminine phrases, which the men condescendingly use to soften our slavish dependence, and despising that weak elegancy of mind, exquisite sensibility, and sweet docility of manners, supposed to be the sexual characteristics of the weaker vessel, I wish to show that elegance is inferior to virtue, that the first object of laudable ambition is to obtain a character as a human being, regardless of the distinction of sex; and that secondary views should be brought to this simple touchstone.

This is a rough sketch of my plan; and should I express my conviction with the energetic emotions that I feel whenever I think of the subject, the dictates of experience and reflection will be felt by some of my readers. Animated by this important object, I shall disdain to cull my phrases or polish my style—I aim at being useful, and sincerity will render me unaffected; for wishing rather to persuade by the force of my arguments, than dazzle by the elegance of my language, I shall not waste my time in rounding periods, nor in fabricating the turgid bombast of artificial feelings, which, coming from the head, never reach the heart. I shall be employed about things, not words! and, anxious to render my sex more respectable members of society, I shall try to avoid that flowery diction which has slided from essays into novels, and from novels into familiar letters and conversation.

These pretty nothings, these caricatures of the real beauty of sensibility, dropping glibly from the tongue, vitiate the taste, and create a kind of sickly delicacy that turns away from simple unadorned truth; and a deluge of false sentiments, and overstretched feelings, stifling the natural emotions of the heart, render the domestic pleasures insipid, that ought to sweeten the exercise of those severe duties, which educate a rational and immortal being for a nobler field of action.

The education of women has, of late, been more attended to than formerly; yet they are still reckoned a frivolous sex, and ridiculed or pitied by the writers who endeavour by satire or instruction to improve them. It is acknowledged that they spend many of the first years of their lives acquiring a smattering of accomplishments: meanwhile, strength of body and mind are sacrificed to libertine notions of beauty, to the desire of establishing themselves, the only way women can rise in the world–by marriage. And this desire making mere animals of them, when they marry, they act as such children may be expected to act: they dress, they paint, and nickname God's creatures. Surely these weak beings are only fit for the seraglio! Can they govern a family, or take care of the poor babes whom they bring into the world?

If then it can be fairly deduced from the present conduct of the sex, from the prevalent fondness for pleasure, which takes place of ambition and those nobler passions that open and enlarge the soul; that the instruction which women have received has only tended, with the constitution of civil society, to render them insignificant objects of desire; mere propagators of fools! if it can be proved, that in aiming to accomplish them, without cultivating their understandings, they are taken out of their sphere of duties, and made ridiculous and useless when the short lived bloom of beauty is over, I presume that *rational* men will excuse me for endeavouring to persuade them to become more masculine and respectable.

Indeed the word masculine is only a bugbear: there is little reason to fear that women will acquire too much courage or fortitude; for their apparent inferiority with respect to bodily strength, must render them, in some degree, dependent of men in the various relations of life; but why should it be increased by prejudices that give a sex to virtue, and confound simple truths with sensual reveries?

Women are, in fact, so much degraded by mistaken notions of female excellence, that I do not mean to add a paradox when I assert, that this artificial weakness produces a propensity to tyrannize, and gives birth to cunning, the natural opponent of strength, which leads them to play off those contemptible infantile airs that undermine esteem even whilst they excite desire. Do not foster these prejudices, and they will naturally fall into their subordinate, yet respectable station in life.

It seems scarcely necessary to say, that I now speak of the sex in general. Many individuals have more sense than their male relatives; and, as nothing preponderates where there is a constant struggle for an equilibrium, without it has naturally more gravity, some women govern their husbands without degrading themselves, because intellect will always govern.

10. "MARRIAGE OF LILLIAN HARMAN AND EDWIN C. WALKER"

MOSES HARMAN

The Pacific Reporter, vol. 13 (March 10–June 16, 1887)

Moses Harman (1830–1910) transformed the small town of Valley Falls, Kansas, into a flashpoint of radical individualism. As the editor for 30 years of the freethought and anarchist paper Lucifer, the Light Bearer, *Harman implemented an "open word" policy that caused him to be harassed for many years by legal authorities. Moreover, though a man of fairly conventional personal ethics, Harman and his circle advocated "free love," by which they meant that sexual relationships should be a matter of personal choice and conscience, absolutely free from the coercive intervention of government. Harman was imprisoned four times for violating obscenity laws. In his final conviction at age 74, he was sentenced to hard labor (breaking rocks) at Joliet Prison.*

Lillian Harman, the daughter of Moses, worked with him on Lucifer, *during which time she met and fell in love with another freethinking anarchist, Edwin C. Walker. In September 1886, apparently as a test of the Kansas marriage statutes, Lillian and Edwin joined in a common law marriage without the involvement of either church or state. After the couple had been arrested and convicted, they appealed the verdict and lost. Imprisonment followed for both Lillian and Edwin. The following document is part of the court transcript from the appeal. It includes a verbatim account of the illegal marriage, as it was originally published in* Lucifer.

Appeal from Jefferson County.

E. C. Walker and Lillian Harman were prosecuted in the district court of Jefferson county for a violation of section 12 of the marriage act, which reads as follows: "That any persons, living together as man and wife, within this state, without being married, shall be deemed guilty of a misdemeanor, and, on conviction thereof, shall be fined in a sum of not less than five hundred dollars, nor more than one thousand dollars, or be imprisoned in the county jail not less than thirty days, nor more than three months." Comp. Laws 1879, p. 539. At the trial, which was had with a jury, Moses Harman, the father of Lillian Harman, testified that on September 19, 1886, his daughter, Lillian, and E.C. Walker entered into what he called an "autonomistic marriage," at his home, in the presence of himself and two other persons. On that occasion, a statement concerning the compact or union about to be entered into was read by the witness, then followed a statement made by E.C. Walker, which was responded to by Lillian Harman, and the ceremony was terminated by another short statement from the witness. These statements were published in the Lucifer, a newspaper edited by the witness, and the account there given was read in evidence, and is as follows:

"Autonomistic Marriage Practicalized.

"While distinctly denying the right of any citizen or citizens, whether minority or majority, to inquire into our private affairs, or to dictate to us as to the manner in which we shall discharge our private duties and obligations to each other, we wish it understood that we are not afraid nor ashamed to let the world know the nature of the civil compact entered into between Lillian Harman and Edwin C. Walker, at the home of the senior editor of 'Lucifer,' on Sunday, the nineteenth of September, 1886, of the common calendar. As our answer, then, to the many questions in regard thereto, we have reproduced as near as possible the aforesaid proceedings.

"(1) M. [Moses] Harman, father of Lillian Harman, one of the parties to this agreement or compact, read the following, as a general statement of principles in regard to marriage: 'Marriage, by which term we mean the various attractions, sentiments, arrangements, and interests, psychical, social, material, involved in the sex-relations of men and women, is, or should be, distinctively a personal matter, a strictly private affair. There are, or should be, but two parties to this arrangement or compact,—a man and a woman; or perhaps we should say, a woman and a man, since the interests, the fate of woman is involved, for weal or woe in marriage, to a far greater extent than is the fate or interests of man. Some one has said, "Marriage is for man only an episode, while for woman it is the epic of her life." Hence it would seem right and proper that, in all arrangements pertaining to marriage, woman should have the first voice or control. Marriage looks to maternity, motherhood, as its most important result or outcome, and, as dame nature has placed the burden of maternity upon woman, it would seem that marriage should be emphatically and distinctively woman's work, woman's institution. It need not be said that this is not the common, the popular, and especially, the legal, view of marriage. The very etymology itself of the word tells a very different story. Marriage is derived from the French word "*mari*," meaning the "husband." And never did the etymology of a word more truly indicate its popular and legal meaning than does the etymology of this one. Marriage, as enforced in so-called Christian lands, as well as in most heathen countries, is pre-eminently man's affair, man's institution. Its origin—mythologic origin—declares that woman was made for man, not man for woman, not each for the other. History shows that man has ruled over woman as mythology declares he should do; and the marriage laws themselves show that they were made by man for man's benefit, not for woman's. Marriage means, or results in, the family as an institution, and the laws and customs pertaining thereto make man the head and autocrat of the family. When a woman marries, she merges her individuality as a legal person into that of her husband, even to the surrender of her name, just as chattel slaves were required to take the name of their master. Against all such invasive laws and unjust discriminations, we, as autonomists, hereby most solemnly protest. We most distinctly and positively reject, repudiate, and abjure all such laws and regulations; and, if we ever have acknowledged allegiance to these statute laws regulating marriage, we hereby renounce and disclaim all such allegiance. To particularize and recapitulate: Marriage being a strictly personal matter, we deny the right of society, in the form of church and state, to regulate it or interfere with the individual man and woman in this relation. All such interference, from our standpoint, is regarded as an impertinence, and worse than an impertinence. To acknowledge the right of the state to dictate to us in these matters is to acknowledge ourselves the children or minor wards of the state, not capable of transacting our own business. We therefore most solemnly and earnestly repudiate, abjure, and reject the authority, the rites, and ceremonies of church and state in marriage, as we reject the mummeries of the church in the ceremony called baptism, and at the bed-side of the dying. The priest, or other state official, can no more prepare the contracting parties for the duties of marriage than he can prepare the dying for life in another world. In either case, the preparation must be the work of the parties immediately concerned. We regard all such attempts at regulation on the part of church and state as not only an impertinence, not only wrong in principle, but disastrous to the last degree in practice. Here, as everywhere else in the realm of personal rights and reciprocal duties, we regard intelligent choice,—untrampled voluntaryism,—coupled with responsibility to natural law for our acts, as the true and only basis of morality. As a matter of principle we are opposed to the making of promises on occasions like this. The promise to "love and honor" may become quite impossible of fulfillment, and that from no fault of the party making such promise. The promise to "love, honor, and obey, so long as both shall live," commonly exacted of woman, we regard as a highly immoral promise. It makes woman the inferior—the vassal—of her husband, and when, from any cause, love ceases to exist between the parties, this promise binds her to do an immoral act, viz: It binds her to prostitute her sex-hood at the command of an unloving and unloveable husband. For these and other reasons that will readily suggest themselves, we, as autonomists, prefer not to make any promises of the kind usually made as part of marriage ceremonies.'

"(2) E. C. Walker, as one of the contracting parties, made the following statement: 'This is a time for clear, frank statement. While regarding all public marital ceremonies as essentially and ineradicably indelicate,—a pandering to the morbid, vicious, and meddlesome element in human nature,—I consider this form the least objectionable. I abdicate in advance all the so-called "marital rights" with which this public acknowledgment of our relationship may invest me. Lillian is and will continue to be as free to repulse any and all advances of mine as she has been heretofore. In joining with me in this love and labor union, she has not alienated a single natural right. She remains sovereign of herself, as I of myself, and we severally and together repudiate all powers legally conferred upon husbands and wives. In legal marriage, woman surrenders herself to the law and to her husband, and becomes a vassal. Here it is different; Lillian is now made free. In brief, and in addition: I cheerfully and distinctly recognize this woman's right to the control of her own person; her right and duty to retain her own name; her right to the possession of all property inherited, earned, or otherwise justly gained by her; her equality with me in this copartnership; my responsibility to her as regards the care of offspring, if any, and her paramount right to the custody thereof, should any unfortunate fate dissolve this union. And now, friends, a few words especially to you. This wholly private compact is here announced, not because I recognize that you, or society at large, or the state, have any right to inquire into or determine our relations to each other, but simply as a guarantee to Lillian of my good faith towards her. And to this I pledge my honor.'

"(3) Lillian Harman then responded as follows: 'I do not care to say much; actions speak more clearly than words, often. I enter into this union with Mr. Walker of my own free will and choice, and I agree with the views of my father and of Mr. Walker as just expressed. I make no promises that it may become impossible or immoral for me to fulfill; but retain the right to act, always, as my conscience and best judgment shall dictate. I retain, also, my full maiden name, as I am sure it is my duty to do. With this understanding, I give to him my hand in token of my trust in him, and of the fidelity to truth and honor of my intentions towards him.'

"Then M. Harman said: 'As the father and natural guardian of Lillian Harman, I hereby give my consent to this union. I do not "give away the bride," as I wish her to be always the owner of her person, and to be free always to act according to her truest and purest impulses, and as her highest judgment may dictate.'"

It was expressly admitted that no license for the marriage of the defendants had been obtained, and that no marriage ceremony was performed by any judge, justice of the peace, or licensed preacher of the gospel, and that neither of the defendants belonged to the society of Friends or Quakers. The proceedings mentioned were followed by the matrimonial cohabitation of the defendants. Upon this testimony, the jury returned a verdict of guilty. Motions in arrest of judgment, and for a new trial, were filed and overruled, and the judgment of the court was that the defendant E. C. Walker be confined in the county jail for a period of 75 days, and the defendant Lillian Harman for a period of 45 days, and that the defendants pay the costs of the action, and stand committed to the jail of the county until payment is made. The defendants appealed.

PART THREE

MORAL INDIVIDUALISM

11. *AN ARROW AGAINST ALL TYRANTS*

RICHARD OVERTON

An Arrow Against All Tyrants and Tyranny, shot from the Prison of Newgate into the Prerogative Bowels of the Arbitrary House of Lords, and All Other Usurpers and Tyrants Whatsoever (1646)
[Spelling and punctuation have been modernized.]

Relatively little is known about the life of Richard Overton (fl. 1631–64). In the 1640s, during the period of the English Civil Wars, he actively participated in the Leveller movement. The Levellers, who were the most consistent libertarians of the 17th century, advocated a wide range of personal and civil liberties, including private property rights, opposition to government monopolies and special privileges, a free press, complete freedom of religion (including freedom for Catholics and atheists), and so forth. The author of many pamphlets on political and religious matters, Overton was imprisoned at least two times, the first of which was from August 1646 to September 1647. It was during this time that Overton wrote An Arrow Against All Tyrants. *This pamphlet is especially noteworthy for its spirited presentation and defense of "self-propriety"—a foundational principle of libertarianism that went by various names, including self-ownership and self-sovereignty.*

Sir,

To every individual in nature is given an individual property by nature, not to be invaded or usurped by any. For every one as he is himself, so he hath a self-propriety, else could he not be himself, and on this no second may presume to deprive any of without manifest violation and affront to the very principles of nature and of the rules of equity and justice between man and man. Mine and thine cannot be except this be: No man hath power over my rights and liberties, and I over no man's. I may be but an individual, enjoy myself and my self-propriety, and may write myself no more than myself, or presume any further; if I do, I am an encroacher and an invader upon another man's right, to which I have no right. For by natural birth, all men are equally and alike born to like propriety, liberty, and freedom. And as we are delivered of God by the hand of nature into this world, every one with a natural, innate freedom and propriety (as it were writ in the table of every man's heart, never to be obliterated), even so are we to live, every one equally and alike to enjoy his birthright and privilege; even all whereof God by nature has made him free.

And this by nature every one desires, aims at, and requires, for no man naturally would be befooled of his liberty by his neighbor's craft or enslaved by his neighbor's might; for it is nature's instinct to preserve itself from all things hurtful and obnoxious, and this in nature is granted of all to be most reasonable, equal, and just, not to be rooted out of the kind, even of equal duration with the creature. And from this fountain or root all just human powers take their original, not immediately from God (as kings usually plead their prerogative) but mediately by the hand of nature, as from the represented to the representers. For, originally, God hath implanted them in the creature, and from the creature those powers immediately proceed, and no further; and no more may be communicated than stands for the better being, weal, or safety thereof. And this is man's prerogative and no further; so much and no more may be given or received thereof, even so much as is conducive to a better being, more safety and freedom, and no more. He that gives more sins against his own flesh, and he that takes more is a thief and robber to his kind. Every man by nature being a king, priest, and prophet in his own natural circuit and compass, whereof no second may partake but by deputation, commission, and free consent from him whose natural right and freedom it is.

And thus, Sir, and no otherwise are you instated into your sovereign capacity for the free people of this nation. For their better being, discipline, government, propriety, and safety have each of them communicated so much unto you (their chosen ones) of their natural rights and powers that you might thereby become their absolute commissioners and lawful deputies, but no more; and that by contraction of those their several individual communications conferred upon and united in you, you alone might become their own natural, proper, sovereign power, therewith singly and only empowered for their several weals, safeties, and freedoms, and no otherwise. For as by nature no man may abuse, beat, torment, or afflict himself, so by nature no man may give that power to another, seeing he may not do it himself; for no more can be communicated from the general than is included in the particulars whereof the general is compounded.

So that [those] so deputed are to the general no otherwise than as a schoolmaster to a particular [or] to this or that man's family. For as such . . . ordering and regulating power is but by deputation . . . and may be removed at the parents' or headmaster's pleasure upon neglect or abuse thereof, and be conferred upon another (no parents ever giving such an absolute, unlimited power to such over their children as to do to them as they list, and not to be retracted, controlled, or restrained in their exorbitances), even so and no otherwise is it with you, our deputies, in respect of the general. It is in vain for you to think you have power over us to save us or destroy us at your pleasure, to do with us as you list, be it for our weal or be it for our woe, and not to be enjoined in mercy to the one or questioned in justice for the other. For the edge of your own arguments against the king in this kind may be turned upon yourselves; for if for the safety of the people he might in equity be opposed by you in his tyrannies, oppressions, and cruelties, even so may you, by the same rule of right reason, be opposed by the people in general in the like cases of destruction and ruin by you upon them. For the safety of the people is the sovereign law to which all must become subject, and for . . . which all powers human are ordained by them. For [all] tyranny, oppression, and cruelty whatsoever, and in whomsoever, is in itself unnatural; illegal, yea, absolutely anti-magisterial, for it is even destructive to all human civil society, and therefore resistible.

Now, Sir, the commons of this nation, having empowered their body representative, whereof you are one, with their own absolute sovereignty, thereby authoritatively and legally to remove from amongst them all oppressions and tyrannies, oppressors, and tyrants, how great soever in name, place, or dignity; and to protect, safeguard, and defend them from all such unnatural monsters, vipers, and pests bred of corruption or which are entrusted amongst them and as much as in them lie, to prevent all such for the future. And to that end you have been assisted with our lives and fortunes most liberally and freely with most victorious and happy success, whereby your arms are strengthened with our might that now you may make us all happy within the confines of this nation, if you please. And therefore, Sir, in reason, equity, and justice, we deserve no less at your hands, and (Sir) let it not seem strange unto you that we are thus bold with you for our own.

For by nature we are the sons of Adam, and from him have legitimately derived a natural propriety, right, and freedom which only we require; and how in equity you can deny us, we cannot see. It is but the just rights and prerogative of mankind (whereunto the people of England are heirs apparent, as well as other nations) which we desire, and surely you will not deny it [to] us that we may be men and live like men. If you do, it will be as little safe for yourselves and posterity as for us and our posterity; for, Sir, [whatever] bondage, thraldom, or tyranny soever you settle upon us, you certainly, or your posterity, will taste of the dregs. If by your present policy and (abused) might, you chance to award it from yourselves in particular, yet your posterity [will] do what you can [and] will be liable to the hazard thereof.

12. FROM *SOCIAL BLISS CONSIDERED*

PETER ANNET

Social Bliss Considered: In Marriage and Divorce; Cohabiting Unmarried, and Public Whoring (London: R. Rose, 1749)
  [Spelling and punctuation have been modernized.]

A *consistent champion of freedom of religion, the deist Peter Annet (1693–1769) transmitted the ideas of freethought to the common people of England. Among his many tracts were* The Resurrection of Jesus Considered, History and Character of Saint Paul, *and* Judging for Ourselves: Or Freethinking the Great Duty of Religion. *"If it not be fit to examine into truth," declared Annet in a passionate appeal common among deists, "truth is not fit to be known." The British government disagreed. For attempting to "diffuse and propagate irreligious and diabolical opinions in the minds of His Majesty's subjects, and to shake the foundation of the Christian religion," Annet, at the advanced age of 70, was pilloried (with a paper on his forehead inscribed "blasphemy") and sentenced to a year of hard labor in prison.*

Our selection is from Annet's most provocative work, Social Bliss Considered, *which was published in 1749 under the pseudonym "Gideon Archer." Annet argues for the legalization of divorce, cohabitation, and prostitution. In the passage excerpted here, from the section titled "Of Public Whoring," Annet argues for the right of adults to consensual sexual activity, without governmental restrictions or punishments. This is an early formulation of the crucial libertarian distinction between vices and crimes.*

Human good and evil, respects human creatures only, and depend on their circumstances. No moral law is absolutely good or evil in all variety of cases; for as the case or circumstance varies, so the good or evil of the action will vary with it. We may not kill, to do it unlawfully is murder; but to kill a criminal, or an enemy in war, is lawful. It is not a crime to eat and drink, unless we do it to excess, and to hurt ourselves, or devour the property of others, and so do hurt to others. Moral good and evil being limited to the nature of man, it must needs be that actions which are injurious to none of the human species, and necessary to be done, because the nature of man requires it, are not evil actions. The action is not evil, which has not evil consequences, whatever the evil was that occasioned it. *By their fruits you shall know them.* What does not injure man cannot displease God. For God governs man by laws for the good of man: God himself is not benefitted or injured by anything that is in the power of man to do because from man God receives nothing. From God man receives all things.

Natural appetites that excite to the propagation and preservation of human life are not in their nature evil to man. Copulation is not an evil in its nature, but in such circumstances as are attended with inconveniency, and some natural bad consequences in body or mind, as in these three particulars:

1. When there is a natural unfitness in the bodily parts nature forbids to join together things unfit to be joined; for it is communicating pain and injury instead of pleasure and gratification. Yet persons may be so unnaturally bound together by the sacred rites, and so disagreeably fitted for the enjoyment of each other.

2. When there is a natural reluctance of one party to comply with the disposition of the other, it is a prohibition of

nature. Whatever is done by one, contrary to the will of the other, or not without *full consent* of both, mars the felicity of enjoyment and is attended with sorrow and grief on one side, as well as compunction and regret on the other, in a temper possessed of humanity. Everything contrary to true harmony is a violation of love and not its offspring. Rapes are of the most brutal nature and deserve severest punishment. To force a virgin, should be esteemed a crime equal to robbing a house. Forced marriages against the good will of both parties, is disagreeable; it is an evil that produces lasting sorrow and unhappiness. The yoking together adverse natures nature forbids. There should be a fitness in body and mind to action to make it fit and agreeable.

3. By dishonorable solicitation, fraudulent insinuation, and false promises, to debauch a mind to an action, the natural consequence of which is injury and repentance, is also criminal. To deflower a virgin under pretense of marriage, and abandon her, is a fraud and knavery; and is naturally productive of ill effects. . . .

These things are evil, because of the injury committed; but the case is different where none are injured, and both parties are free and pleased with each other's actions and are under no engagements of restraint than their own nature and common prudence direct. I see no reason why persons that are at their own disposal have not as much natural right to dispose of their own persons according to their own pleasure as of their substance, income, or estate if the one be as much their property as the other. If it be not so, then people dare not for their soul's sake say their bodies are their own; but if it be so, it is not evident why they ought to be punished for disposing of themselves as they please, especially when matrimony, as it now is, is often worse, or of more fatal consequence; nor will it ever be esteemed honorable by those that are unhappy, while the means of happiness are withheld. . . .

It is well known that in the satisfying of every natural desire of man, especially those that give the most delight, nature needs a bridle not a spur; because more are injured by too great freedom than restraint. Therefore prudence steers the middle way, and therefore reason is given to regulate our desires. Yet the moderate gratification of what nature makes necessary can be no crime, when the property of none is invaded, and none are injured by it. It is only the immoderate use of pleasure or seeking it to the detriment of others that makes it criminal. Therefore this can be no reason to use a muzzle instead of a bridle, nor to make those actions criminal that are the incitements of innocent nature, which she alone ripens man for, and constrains his will to desire. And he cannot help desiring what she fits him to enjoy and which not nature but custom makes criminal. For how can they be culpable of committing evil to others who neither do nor intend any? And man or woman cannot will evil to themselves; for evil consists in grief and pain. The gratification of every sense contributes to the pleasure of life or man's well-being, and every sense was given to man for that end to be enjoyed within the bounds of reason in proper circumstances; and those circumstances are proper and reasonable that are by joint consent and hurtful to none. Pleasures enjoyed and communicated prudently within natural and reasonable bounds and with necessary regard to health and substance, so as not to be attended with the apprehension of guilt, or the fear of after-pain, are enjoyed with satisfaction. What makes pleasure the greater to an honest mind is to be satisfied with reason how it may be enjoyed so as not to disturb the mind's felicity by self-accusation or after-reflections. For the pleasures of sense are marred if the fruition is not with the full satisfaction of mind that a good understanding and a prudent conduct are always necessary to promote.

As to eat to satisfy hunger makes not the action evil—for were it not for this men would have no desire to eat nor find pleasure in eating, consequently could not eat at all—so the gratification of carnal lust to the injury of none, is no evil; nor is the lust or desire itself, for were it not for that, (to which nature has joined love to the object to enforce it) all procreation and the pleasures and virtues of a social life and family relations would be at an end. Therefore, barely *to look on a woman to lust after her*, without some other explanatory words, *is not committing adultery in heart*. It is not an evil, because unavoidable, and sometimes necessary. If carnal lust be in itself an evil motive, it must be so at all times, or in all cases, and consequently is so in a married state. For in this case marriage doesn't change the motive to the action; if it did, it would either be not done at all, or be very ill done. It is not evil to gratify the natural lusts of sense by which life and being are supported and propagated; but to do it to the prejudice of others. Where neither party injure each other, but a man's natural appetite is satisfied by the use of an obliging courtesan, if he is under no legal ties to another that ought in reason to restrain him, but pleasure is mutually given and received, I cannot see any evil to be in the action more than in the desire, which desires being infused by nature for the good of man, vigorous in the best, and unavoidable in all in whom they are, which man's will or wisdom cannot prevent, are not evil. Although through the mist of false divinity they be made to appear, and be accounted so. It is the forbidding it makes it criminal or rather to be esteemed as such: For this desire does not arise from a vicious and corrupted mind, but is the genuine offspring of pure nature in the purest minds.

13. FROM "VICES ARE NOT CRIMES: A VINDICATION OF MORAL LIBERTY"

LYSANDER SPOONER

Prohibition a Failure, or The True Solution of the Temperance Question,
Dio Lewis (Boston: James R. Osgood and Co., 1875)

Lysander Spooner (1808–87) was an American lawyer, abolitionist, and radical libertarian who maintained that governments should be strictly limited to protecting the natural rights of individuals. The essay from which our excerpt was taken, Spooner's Vices Are Not Crimes, *was first published anonymously in 1875 as a chapter in a book titled* Prohibition a Failure *by the physician Dio Lewis. Spooner's authorship remained generally unknown until after his death, when Benjamin Tucker mentioned it in his memorial of Spooner, which was published in the anarchist periodical* Liberty.

Spooner argues that vices "are simply the errors which a man makes in his search after his own happiness," whereas crimes are actions that violate the rights of other people. He concludes that any effort to prohibit personal vices through the force of law is hypocritical, counter-productive, and profoundly unjust.

I

Vices are those acts by which a man harms himself or his property.

Crimes are those acts by which one man harms the person or property of another.

Vices are simply the errors which a man makes in his search after his own happiness. Unlike crimes, they imply no malice toward others, and no interference with their persons or property.

In vices, the very essence of crime—that is, the design to injure the person or property of another—is wanting.

It is a maxim of the law that there can be no crime without a criminal intent; that is, without the intent to invade the person or property of another. But no one ever practises a vice with any such criminal intent. He practises his vice for his own happiness solely, and not from any malice toward others.

Unless this clear distinction between vices and crimes be made and recognized by the laws, there can be on earth no such thing as individual right, liberty, or property; no such things as the right of one man to the control of his own person and property, and the corresponding and co-equal rights of another man to the control of his own person and property.

For a government to declare a vice to be a crime, and to punish it as such, is an attempt to falsify the very nature of things. It is as absurd as it would be to declare truth to be falsehood, or falsehood truth.

II

Every voluntary act of a man's life is either virtuous or vicious. That is to say, it is either in accordance, or in conflict, with those natural laws of matter and mind, on which his physical, mental, and emotional health and well-being depend. In other words, every act of his life tends, on the whole, either to his happiness, or to his unhappiness. No single act in his whole existence is indifferent.

Furthermore, each human being differs in his physical, mental, and emotional constitution, and also in the circumstances by which he is surrounded, from every other human being. Many acts, therefore, that are virtuous, and tend to happiness, in the case of one person, are vicious, and tend to unhappiness, in the case of another person.

Many acts, also, that are virtuous, and tend to happiness, in the case of one man, at one time, and under one set of circumstances, are vicious, and tend to unhappiness, in the case of the same man, at another time, and under other circumstances.

I I I

To know what actions are virtuous, and what vicious—in other words, to know what actions tend, on the whole, to happiness, and what to unhappiness— in the case of each and every man, in each and all the conditions in which they may severally be placed, is the profoundest and most complex study to which the greatest human mind ever has been, or ever can be, directed. It is, nevertheless, the constant study to which each and every man—the humblest in intellect as well as the greatest— is *necessarily driven* by the desires and necessities of his own existence. It is also the study in which each and every person, from his cradle to his grave, must necessarily form his own conclusions; because no one else knows or feels, or can know or feel, as he knows and feels, the desires and necessities, the hopes, and fears, and impulses of his own nature, or the pressure of his own circumstances.

I V

It is not often possible to say of those acts that are called vices, that they really are vices, *except in degree*. That is, it is difficult to say of any actions, or courses of action, that are called vices, that they really would have been vices, *if they had stopped short of a certain point*. The question of virtue or vice, therefore, in all such cases, is a question of quantity and degree, and not of the intrinsic character of any single act, by itself. This fact adds to the difficulty, not to say the impossibility, of any one's—except each individual for himself—drawing any accurate line, or anything like any accurate line, between virtue and vice; that is, of telling where virtue ends, and vice begins. And this is another reason why this whole question of virtue and vice should be left for each person to settle for himself.

V

Vices are usually pleasurable, at least for the time being, and often do not disclose themselves as vices, by their effects, until after they have been practised for many years; perhaps for a lifetime. To many, perhaps most, of those who practise them, they do not disclose themselves as vices at all during life. Virtues, on the other hand, often appear so harsh and rugged, they require the sacrifice of so much present happiness, at least, and the results, which alone prove them to be virtues, are often so distant and obscure, in fact, so absolutely invisible to the minds of many, especially of the young, that, from the very nature of things, there can be no universal, or even general, knowledge that they are virtues. In truth, the studies of profound philosophers have been expended—if not wholly in vain, certainly with very small re-sults—in efforts to draw the lines between the virtues and the vices.

If, then, it be so difficult, so nearly impossible, in most cases, to determine what is, and what is not, vice; and especially if it be so difficult, in nearly all cases, to determine where virtue ends, and vice begins; and if these questions, which no one can really and truly determine for anybody but himself, are not to be left free and open for experiment by all, each person is deprived of the highest of all his rights as a human being, to wit: his right to inquire, investigate, reason, try experiments, judge, and ascertain for himself, what is, *to him*, virtue, and what is, *to him*, vice; in other words, what, on the whole, conduces to *his* happiness, and what, on the whole, conduces to *his* unhappiness. If this great right is not to be left free and open to all, then each man's whole right, as a reasoning human being, to "liberty and the pursuit of happiness," is denied him.

14. "ARCHBISHOP TEMPLE ON BETTING"

HENRY WILSON

The Liberty Review, June 15, 1901

Henry Wilson, a lieutenant colonel in the British army, was a frequent contributor to The Liberty Review *(published by the Liberty and Property Defence League), until he was killed in a bicycle accident on January 8, 1907. He was secretary of the Individualist Club, treasurer of the Personal Rights Association, and a contributor to Auberon Herbert's periodical titled* Free Life. *In this article, Wilson comments both on the moral double standard that was used when assessing different economic classes and on the uselessness of vice legislation.*

We all remember the French nobleman whose life had not been a pattern of morality, but who said, when dying, that he had no doubt the Almighty would make due allowance for the fact that he was a gentleman, and would not be so hard on his peccadilloes as if he were a plebeian. The Archbishop of Canterbury seems to share this feeling, for he said (on May 20th, in the House of Lords) that betting was certainly a vice when practised by those who could not afford it. There are some men so strong that drunkenness does not seem to affect them—so, of course, in them, it ceases to be a vice. When Captain Yelverton was asked, at the Longworth trial, if he thought seduction was wrong, he said it depended on the social position of the girl. *Punch,* years ago, had an amusing cartoon, representing John Thomas lounging in his mistress's carriage and consulting his betting book. To me it seems no more blamable in a footman, who is an idle person, to fill up the vacuity in his mind in that way than it is in his master. Gambling is, of course, an inheritance from our savage ancestors, who, having no subjects of interest to think about, killed time in that way, as savages do now all over the world. We ought, by this time, to have got rid of the pestilent heresy that wealth and position give us more licence to indulge in idleness and vice than people in a humbler station. Virtue and vice ought to be independent of station or sex. There is nothing wonderful in the Bishops of Hereford and London interfering. What good can a Select Committee do? Betting has increased because more people read the papers and wages have risen, just as smoking has increased among boys since cigarettes have become common. The facts are all well known, and a Committee can throw no new light on the subject. The Bishops say that public opinion will be aroused. Let public opinion direct itself to the rich first, and not wink at the betting ring on racehorses or gambling at the clubs in Pall Mall while sanctioning raids on clubs of tailors and butchers, or on men who bet in shillings at street corners. It is very amusing to hear the Bishop of Hereford say that *moderate* legislation on this subject was not open to the same objection as legislation in restriction of the drink traffic, or on the hours of shop assistants. It is something to hear a confession that legislation on the latter subjects is bad; but there is still the delusion that a little of a bad thing is a good thing, and that law can alter men's hearts.

15. FROM *VOLUNTARY SOCIALISM*

FRANCIS DASHWOOD TANDY

Voluntary Socialism (Denver: Francis D. Tandy Publisher, 1896)

This selection is from Francis Tandy's provocative, self-published book titled Voluntary Socialism. *Like Benjamin Tucker and other individualist–anarchists of his day, Tandy sometimes used the word "socialism" to mean a system of voluntary social cooperation, or "voluntaryism," in contrast to "state socialism." One of the few modern writers to mention Tandy was Robert Nozick, in* Anarchy, State, and Utopia. *Nozick included Tandy's name in a list of individualist–anarchists who advocated competing protection and justice agencies instead of a sovereign, monopolistic government. Economist and historian Murray Rothbard subsequently became the best known proponent of this type of free-market anarchism, a position that remains popular among some modern libertarians.*

In this selection from Voluntary Socialism, *Tandy presents a theory of egoism that was based on the ideas of Max Stirner. Contrary to many negative interpretations of "survival of the fittest," Tandy maintains that this process requires a high degree of individual freedom and social diversity, that it recognizes "the welfare of the individual to be of paramount importance," and that it will result in the general welfare. It should also be noted that Tandy was a social determinist, as were many of his anarchist contemporaries.*

The term "survival of the fittest"—first used by Spencer and afterwards endorsed by Darwin—is in many respects more exact, but even it is not proof against the carelessness of the untrained mind. A large number of people think that the "fittest" are those individuals who best conform to their standard of ethics. The word is only used to signify those who can best adapt themselves to their environment. It is easy to see that in a country where food is scarce those individuals who had religious objections to killing and eating their aged parents would stand a poorer chance of surviving than their less punctilious brethren. In this case the cannibals would be the fittest to survive, while, judged from our ethical standpoint, the others would probably be considered more moral. . . .

The survival of the fittest must of necessity remain inoperative until a certain amount of variation exists. If all individuals were alike there could be no "fittest" to survive. The smaller the amount of this variation, the slower must the change be. Thus the species which manifests the greatest variety among its individuals is most likely to adapt itself quickly to changed conditions. Any species in which variation is unknown and which has become a fixed type must suffer total extinction if its environments change. The only reason the lowest forms of life have continued to exist, in spite of almost universal change, is that the changed conditions do not affect their limited environments and so "the species remains constant."

Selection pre-supposes variation and operates only through the most relentless competition. By the extinction of those individuals which are least able to adapt themselves to their environment, the species develops those characteristics which have proved beneficial to the surviving individuals.

Applying these conclusions to social reform, we see that permanent improvement in human society can only be found under conditions which are favorable to the development of different characteristics among its members, which recognize the welfare of the individual to be of paramount importance and which foster the freest competition in order that welfare may become general.

The foolish philanthropy so prevalent to-day, which would prevent the pro-creation of the unfit and which seeks to lessen competition, must be unqualifiedly condemned. To limit the number of births, even of criminals, is to limit the variation of the species. Any such action makes the perfect adaptation of us to our environments less speedy and less sure. The wider the variation the greater chance is there for the production of favorable types. Then competition is absolutely essential in order to weed out the unfit and to make the variation beneficial to the race. It is impossible for a few self-conceited lady novelists to tell what individuals will prove the fittest, or what combination is necessary to produce such individuals. If the teachings of evolution are true, all external force which limits the pro-creation of any individuals—whether good or bad—or restricts competition must result disastrously to the human race.

From this standpoint the present social system is condemned on every hand. It places a special premium upon one characteristic—the ability to get money—at the expense of every other. It fosters a spirit of self-sacrificing patriotism and so places the welfare of the country above that of the individual. It denies the first essential of free competition—the right of every individual to the free use of the earth—and hedges us around with restrictions of all kinds. Unfortunately most of the proposed reforms seek to intensify these evils instead of to remove them. . . .

The habits of the lower animals, the growth and development of plants and the motion of the heavenly bodies may all be generalized, and the laws in accordance with which they act may be stated. May not the motives of human action be also subject to generalization? This is a question to which the old school of philosophers gives a negative, the modern school, an affirmative answer.

The fact that a person reads or writes a book devoted to social science pre-supposes an agreement with the modern idea. It is only when human action is generalized that a science of society can be found possible. Such a science must consist of generalizations of human action and deductions from those generalizations. If men are "free moral agents," that is, if they can act of their own volition regardless of the rest of the universe, any generalization of their actions is impossible. Even if under such conditions any general statement of their past actions could be made, it would be valueless, for there would be no guarantee that they would again act in a similar manner under similar circumstances. Anyone that admits the possibility of a social science is thereby committed to the doctrine of necessity, that is, that a certain individual, placed in certain environments, of necessity acts in a certain manner. This being assumed, it becomes of the very first importance to discover the fundamental law of human action, for on this law all sound theories of social reform must depend.

The Theist declares that we should always act in accordance with the commands of God. Admitting, for the sake of argument, the existence of God, why should we obey Him? Immediately the answer suggests itself. God being the supreme ruler of the universe, it is the height of folly to antagonize Him. He can heap disasters from which there is no escape on those who disobey Him, and is capable of rewarding with eternal joy those who uphold His honor and glory. We must obey the commands of God and deny ourselves in this life, in order that we may reap joys eternal. "Lay not up for yourselves treasures upon the earth; where rust and moth doth corrupt, and where thieves break through and steal: but lay up for yourselves treasures in heaven; where neither rust nor moth do corrupt, and where thieves do not break through and steal." This is the essence of the Christian religion.

The Altruist maintains that we should love our fellow man and act for his good. If we love our fellow man, the sight of pain in him will make us unhappy and his happiness will cause us pleasure. So we proceed to ameliorate his pain and increase his happiness in order that we ourselves may be happy. But why should I love my fellow man? If I don't love him or feel badly when he suffers, I certainly will not put myself to the trouble of helping him, unless I know that he will help me in turn when I shall need it.

"You should act for the greatest good of the community," says another. Why should you, except in so far as the good of the community is liable to result in good to you? Even if you owe the community anything, why should you pay? Still the same answer, "If you don't it will be the worse for you."

But now up comes another and says, "You must act from a sense of duty." Duty to whom? To God? I owe Him only such obedience as He gains through my fear of punishment or hope of reward. To my neighbor? What do I owe him? Only that consideration which we agree to accord each other for our mutual good. To society? To my family? To the state? The same answer applies. Turn which way you will, the idea of duty entirely disappears.

John Stuart Mill says, "The internal sanction of duty, whatever our standard of duty may be, is . . . a feeling in our own mind; a pain, more or less intense, attendant on violations of duty, which in properly cultivated moral natures rises, in the most serious cases, into shrinking from it as an impossibility. . . . Its binding force, however, consists in the existence of a mass of feelings which must be broken through in order to do what violates our standard of right, and which, if we do nevertheless violate that standard, will probably have to be encountered afterwards in the form of remorse." Thus there are two forces which cause us to pursue a right course of action, the external force or fear of retaliation, and the internal force or fear of our conscience.

The conscience has been considered by many as the distinctive attribute of man—the spark divine in the human breast. Darwin, however, found many evidences of it in the lower animals. Really there is nothing mysterious about it. "At the moment of action man will no doubt be apt to follow the stronger impulse; and though this may occasionally prompt him to the noblest deeds, it will more commonly lead him to gratify his own desires at the expense of other men. But after their gratification, when past and weaker impressions are judged by the ever-enduring social instinct, and by his deep regard for the good opinion of his fellows, retribution will surely come. He will then feel remorse, repentance, regret or shame; this latter feeling, however, relates almost exclusively to the judgment of others. He will consequently resolve more or less firmly to act differently for the future; and this is conscience; for the conscience looks backward and serves as a guide for the future."

We must by no means underestimate the important part which this internal force plays in deciding the happiness or unhappiness of most men. But both the internal and the external forces, which deter us from a wrong course of action, operate upon our knowledge that such a course will ultimately result in unhappiness. This is the only ultimate motive of action.

If every individual always attempts to attain the greatest amount of happiness, the doctrine of Necessity follows as a logical deduction. Given a complete knowledge of all the environments in which an individual is placed and a complete knowledge of that individual's conception of happiness (this latter includes an exact idea of his intelligence) and we could determine with mathematical certainty what course of action he would pursue. That this exactness is never reached is due to the practical impossibility of obtaining all the necessary data. But it is surprising how accurate the keen observer of human nature often is in foreseeing the actions of another. This accuracy will be found to increase or diminish in proportion as more or less correct estimates of the actor's character and environments are formed. Conan Doyle gives us a glimpse of the possibilities in this line in his famous Sherlock Holmes stories.

If, on the other hand, men do not always act from motives of self interest, but sometimes from selfish and sometimes from unselfish motives, it is impossible to generalize their conduct in the slightest. In which case, as above stated, a science of society is absolutely unthinkable. The absurdity of such a position need hardly be pointed out, in spite of the voluminous works which have been written in its defence. So we are justified in maintaining that all action resolves itself into an attempt on the part of an organism to place itself in harmony with its environments; that is, to increase its happiness or, what is the same thing, to decrease its pain. Such is the philosophy of Egoism.

This is the only theory of psychology which is in harmony with the doctrine of evolution, for it is a *sine qua non* of that competition which is so essential to natural and sexual selection.

In accordance with this principle all our actions may be divided into two classes: those from which we expect to derive pleasure directly, and those from which, though often unpleasant in themselves, we hope ultimately to gain more happiness than pain. When a man goes for a walk on a pleasant afternoon, he expects to derive pleasure from the walk. But when, on a cold, wintry night, he walks several miles through the snow to go to a dance, the walk becomes only a means to attain happiness; in other words, he sacrifices his immediate pleasure for one which is greater though more remote. The two possible courses of action are perpetually conflicting with one another. We pursue one course or the other, according as our experience and intelligence may prompt us.

So many of our actions are the result of sacrificing the immediate to the remoter pleasure, that people begin to look upon that sacrifice as something noble, forgetful of the fact that it is only a means to attain greater happiness in the end. Experience teaches us that it is often advisable to sacrifice minor points for the benefit of others, in order that we may either escape the pain of self-reproach, or that we may reasonably expect others to help us when we shall need it. This is a purely Egoistic course of action. We can often perform great services for others at the cost of very little trouble to ourselves, and we often need assistance which others can give us without much inconvenience, but which is invaluable to us. These exchanges are for mutual benefit. When people lose sight of that mutual benefit and say we must sacrifice ourselves without any hope of reward, they get altogether beyond the pale of reason.

If self-sacrifice is good, the more we have of it the better, and the man who gives away all that he has except just enough to keep him alive is the finest member of society. But now a paradox is manifest. If the self-sacrificer is the noblest member of society, the one who accepts that sacrifice is the meanest. So to manifest due humility we should debase ourselves by permitting others to sacrifice themselves for our good. This nice little piece of jugglery may be kept up *ad infinitum*. A can sacrifice himself, by permitting B to sacrifice himself, by condescending to allow A to sacrifice himself, and so on as long as you like.

If self-sacrifice is good, to sacrifice oneself for the benefit of the lower animals, from whom no return of the kindness can be reasonably expected, is still better. Since we cannot even breathe, much less eat, drink or be clothed, without destroying life, suicide becomes the only moral course. Now the same old paradox confronts us again. The fulfilment of duty is a source of happiness from which the self-sacrificer should flee. Instead of committing suicide as in duty bound, he should live to kill others. Mental gymnastics of this nature may be highly amusing, but they are hardly satisfactory when offered as a substitute for a philosophical system. Yet this is all the self-sacrifice theory, or Altruism, as it is called, has to offer. It is absurd whichever way it is approached. . . .

. . . It requires but little imagination to trace the effect of the spirit of utilitarianism operating upon this useless self-immolation and transforming it into the modern idea of self-sacrifice. People often find it necessary to submit to temporary pain in order to gain more permanent happiness. Gradually the cake of custom hardens. The means are mistaken for the end, and the whole trend of human thought is perverted in consequence.

Egoism, as such, does not teach us how to act. It simply states why we act as we do. It is merely an analysis of the motives of action, but on the result of this analysis all true ethics must rest. In declaring that all action is the result of an attempt on the part of the individual to secure the greatest possible happiness, the Egoist merely asserts a fact. Having discovered this fact, he will base a theory of conduct upon it, with the end in view of obtaining the greatest amount of happiness. He will sacrifice an immediate pleasure for one more remote when it seems good to him, and not when it appears otherwise. Thus he says to himself, "I will countenance the killing of animals for my food, because the good to be derived from so doing is greater than the disadvantages. But I will discountenance unnecessary cruelty; first because cruelty to animals makes a man brutal in his nature, and such a man is liable to injure me or some one I love; secondly, because the sight, or even the thought, of unnecessary pain is unpleasant to me; and thirdly, because I derive no benefit from it.

So with regard to all his actions with other men, after taking into consideration the feelings of satisfaction or remorse he will experience from a certain act, the chances of the action exciting the resentment or commendation of the rest of the community, and the effect of setting an example which is liable to be followed by someone else to-morrow and cause a similar course of action to be applied to him, after taking all these and similar factors into consideration, he will, if he be a wise man, be governed by the highest expediency. . . .

If all our acts are attempts to gain greater happiness, it behoves us to exert all our energies to the attainment of that end. This gives us a direct rational basis of ethics. The idea of duty is absolutely lost. Actions appear to be good only insofar as they minister to our happiness, and bad insofar as they cause us pain. The term right is synonymous with wise, and wrong, with foolish.

The highest morality is to devote all our efforts to attainment of happiness, leaving others free to do the same. The golden rule must be stated negatively and made to read, "Mind your own business." As Egoists we are bound to assume that others are seeking their own greatest happiness, and as long as they do this, it is impertinent to interfere with them and foolish to set an example which will probably be followed and result in interference with our own affairs. If others attempt to meddle with us, we are justified in acting towards them in such a manner that they will find the pain resulting from such a course far outweighs the pleasure and, consequently, will not be tempted to repeat the experiment.

The Egoist should abstain from all interference with others and resent any similar liberties they may take with him. He is not even justified in meddling with another's business for his good. He is bound to assume that everyone is wise enough to know what constitutes his own happiness. If he isn't, he will suffer the consequences and know better next time.

Every individual should be brought to understand that he is responsible for his actions and will suffer the consequences of all his mistakes. This is really inevitable. The attempt to evade the law of individual responsibility invariably results disastrously. It leads people to suppose that they can act foolishly and not suffer the consequences, and when their folly finds them out there is no one to help them. The doctrine of individual responsibility is a corollary of Egoism. It teaches self-reliance instead of self-sacrifice, dependence upon self instead of upon others. To develop this feeling it is only necessary to give people a chance to practice it. To say that I am my brother's keeper, is to admit that he is also mine. Devote yourself to being happy and I will do the same. If we all succeed the social question will be solved. If we fail, let us try again with our intelligence improved by past experience. "Enlightenment makes selfishness useful and this usefulness popular."

16. FROM *TRUE CIVILIZATION*

JOSIAH WARREN

True Civilization: An Immediate Necessity, and the Last Ground of Hope for Mankind (Boston: J. Warren, 1868)

The American libertarian Josiah Warren (1798–1874) was a musician and an inventor before turning to social reform under the influence of Robert Owen. In 1825, Warren moved with his family to New Harmony, Indiana, to join the first Owenite community in the United States. Although Warren became disillusioned with some of Owen's ideas, his passion for social reform endured. Warren popularized, if he did not actually coin, the expression "self-sovereignty" among American and British individualists, including J. S. Mill. Although commonly called "the first American anarchist," Warren never applied that label to himself.

In our excerpt from True Civilization: An Immediate Necessity, and the Last Ground of Hope for Mankind, *we have omitted Warren's discussion of the labor theory of value. We have focused instead on his belief that the self-sovereignty of voluntary individualism is the foundation of a peaceful social order.*

---

1. With all due deference to other judgments I venture to assert that our present deplorable condition, like that of many other parts of the world, is in consequence of the people in general never having perceived, or else having lost sight of, the legitimate object of all governments as displayed or implied in the American "Declaration of Independence."

2. Every individual of mankind has an "INALIENABLE right to Life, Liberty, and the pursuit of Happiness;" "and it is solely to *protect* and *secure* the enjoyment of these rights unmolested that governments can properly be instituted among men." In other terms, SELF-SOVEREIGNTY is an instinct of every living organism; and it being an *instinct*, cannot be alienated or separated from that organism. It is the instinct of Self-Preservation; the votes of ten thousand men cannot alienate it from a single individual, nor could the bayonets of twenty thousand men neutralize it in any one person any more than they could put a stop to the in-stinctive desire for food in a hungry man.

3. The action of this instinct being INVOLUNTARY, every one has the same absolute right to its exercise that he has to his complexion or the forms of his features, to any extent, not disturbing another; and it is solely to prevent or restrain such disturbances or encroachments, that governments are properly instituted. In still shorter terms, the legitimate and appropriate mission of governments is the defence and pro-tection of the inalienable right of *Sovereignty* in every indi-vidual within his or her own sphere. . . .

7. The instinct of self-preservation or self-sovereignty is not the work of man; but to keep it constantly in mind as a sacred right in all human intercourse is highly expedient.

8. Perceiving that we can invent nothing higher than expedi-ents, we necessarily set aside all imperative or absolute authorities, all sanguinary and unbending codes, creeds, and theories, and leave every one *Free* to choose among expedients: or, in other words, we place all action upon the *voluntary* basis. Do not be alarmed, we shall see this to be the highest expedient whenever it is possible.

9. It is only when the voluntary is wantonly encroached upon, that the employment of force is expedient or justifiable.

10. It appears, however, that no rule or law can be laid down to determine beforehand, what will constitute an offensive encroachment—what one will resist another will excuse, and the subtle *diversities* of different persons and cases, growing out of the inherent individualities of each, have defied all attempts at perfect formulizing excepting this of the *Sovereignty of every individual over his or her own*; and even this must be violated in resisting its violation!

11. The legitimate sphere of every individual has never been publicly determined; but until it is clearly defined, we can never tell what constitutes encroachment— what may be safely excused, or what may be profitably resisted.

12. We will attempt then to define the sphere within which every individual may legitimately, rightly exercise *supreme* power or absolute authority. This sphere would include his or her person, time, property, and responsibilities.

13. By the word right is meant simply that which necessarily tends towards the end in view—the end in view here is permanent and universal peace, and security of person and property.

14. I have said (in effect) that the present confusion and widespread violence and destruction result from a want of appreciation of this great right of Individual Sovereignty, and its defence by government.

15. I now proceed to illustrate and prove this by considering what would be the natural consequences of bearing these two ideas all the time in mind as the regulators of political and moral movements, and holding them, as it were, as

substitutes for all previous laws, customs, precedents, and theories.

16. First, then, while admitting this right of Sovereignty in every one, I shall not be guilty of the ill manners of attempting to *offensively* enforce any of my theoretical speculations, which has been the common error of all governments! This itself would be an attempted encroachment that would justify resistance.

17. The whole mission of coercive government being the defence of persons and property against offensive encroachments, it must have force enough for the purpose. This force necessarily resolves itself into the military, for the advantages of drill and systematic co-operation: and this being perhaps the best form that *government* can assume, while a coercive force is needed, I make no issue with it but only with the misapplications of its immense power.

18. Adhering closely to the idea of *restraining violence* as the mission of government or military power, if this *sole* purpose was instilled into the general mind as an element of education or discipline, no force could be raised to *invade* any persons or property whatever, and no defence would be necessary. . . .

21. *Every* person being entitled to *sovereignty* within his own sphere, there can be, consistently, no limits or exceptions to the title to protection in the legitimate exercise of this sacred right, whether on this side or the other side of the Atlantic, and whether "in a state of war" or not: and, as soon as we take position for this universal right for all the world, we shall have all the world *for* us and *with* us and no enemies to contend with. Did military men ever think of this? Did governments ever think of it?

22. The whole proper business of government is the restraining offensive encroachments, or unnecessary violence to persons and property, or enforcing compensation therefor: but if, in the exercise of this power, we commit an unnecessary violence to *any person whatever or to any property*, we, ourselves, have become the aggressors, and should be resisted.

23. But who is to decide *how much* violence is *necessary* in any given case? We here arrive at the pivot upon which all power now turns for good or evil; this pivot, under formal, exacting, aggressive institutions or *constitutions*, is the person who decides as to their meaning. If one decides for all, then all but that one are, perhaps, enslaved; if each one's title to Sovereignty is admitted, there will be different interpretations, and this *freedom to differ* will ensure emancipation, safety, repose, even in a political atmosphere! and all the cooperation we ought to expect will come from the coincidence of motives according to the merits of each case as estimated by different minds. Where there is evidence of aggression palpable to all minds, all might co-operate to resist it: and where the case is not clearly made out, there will be more or less hesitation: Two great nations will not then be so *very* ready to jump at each other's throats when the most cunning lawyers are puzzled to decide which is wrong!

24. Theorize as we may about the interpretation of "the Constitution," every individual *does* unavoidably measure it and all other words by his own peculiar understanding or conceits, whether he understands himself or not, and should, like General Jackson, recognize the fact, "take responsibility of it," and qualify himself to meet its consequences. The full appreciation of this simple but almost

unknown fact will neutralize the war element in all verbal controversies, and the binding power of all indefinite words, and place conformity thereto on the voluntary basis! Did any institution-makers (except the signers of the "Declaration") ever think of this?. . .

36. Admitting this indestructible right of Sovereignty in *every Individual, at all times and in all conditions*, one will not attempt to *govern* (but only guide or lead) another; but we shall trust to principle or *purpose* for a general and voluntary coincidence and co-operation. Military officers will then become directors or leaders—*not "commanders"*—obedience will be all the more prompt because it is rendered for *an object*—the greatest that can inspire human action, RESISTANCE TO ALL ATTEMPTS AT OFFENSIVE AND UNNECESSARY GOVERNING OR ENCROACHMENTS upon ANY persons or property whatsoever, as the great guarantee for the security of each and every individual. Then every Man, Woman, and Child in the world is interested in acting for and with such a government! . . .

48. If we have been correct in our reasonings, then we have found the clue to the true mission and form of Government—To the most perfect, yet harmless subordination—The reconciliation of obedience with FREEDOM—To the cessation of all hostilities between parties and Nations—To universal co-operation for universal preservation and security of persons and property. We have found a government, literally *in* the people, *of* the people, *for* the people—a government that *is* the people: for Men, Women, and Children can take some direct or indirect part in it—a ready police or army adapted to all demands for either—a self-protecting *"Party of the whole."*

49. A "Union" not only on paper, but rooted in the heart—whose members, trained in the constant reverence for the "inalienable right" of Sovereignty in every person, would be habituated to forbearance towards even wrong opinions and different educations and tastes, to patient endurance of irremediable injuries, and a self-governing deportment and gentleness of manner, and a prompt but careful resistance to wanton aggression wherever found, which would meet with a ready and an affectionate welcome in any part of the world.

50. Every intelligent person would wish to be a member or to contribute, in some manner, to the great common cause.

51. No coercive system of taxation could be necessary to such a government! A government so simple that children will be first to comprehend it, and which even they can see it for their interests to assist. . . .

76. This absolute right of *Sovereignty* in every individual, over his or her *person, time, and property* is the only rule or principle known to this writer that is not subject to exceptions and failures as a regulator of human intercourse. . . .

86. It will be seen, by some at least, that each individual assuming his or *her* share of the deciding power or government as proposed, the great "American idea" may be practically realized; and that the ever-disturbing problem of the "balance of political power" becomes solved, and security for person and property (the great proposed object of all governments) prospectively attained.

87. If others see in this only the "inauguration of Anarchy," let no attempt be made to urge them into conformity, but let them *freely and securely* await the results of demonstration. . . .

475. With regard to a "wild pursuit after a distorted Freedom," nothing has ever so effectually restrained and regulated the

instinctive and impulsive pursuit of our own ends, and invested Freedom with such beautiful and enchanting symmetry as the sacred and constant regard to this absolute right of *unqualified* sovereignty in others over their own; and so inspires a ready spirit of forbearance and accommodation where the mutual exercise of this divine *absolute right* is impossible; and the most polite, benevolent, Equitable, charming deportment in the highest cultivated circles, is characterized in every step, word, and deed, as if this idea was the divine regulator of all.

476. The great difficulty has been in determining *what constitutes one's own,* over which he *may* harmlessly exercise this unqualified jurisdiction, or sovereignty, especially with regard to property. . . .

478. It is possible that the sphere of individual absolute jurisdiction has not been fully and exactly stated, but if each one becomes so *conditioned* that he can exercise this jurisdiction over his or her own person, responsibilities, time, and property, without disturbing others, true order will have commenced, and future wisdom may supply deficiencies.

479. "INDIVIDUALITY" has been misapprehended and misrepresented as "isolation," "selfishness," "unsociableness," etc.

480. I say *misapprehended,* because I cannot believe that any one who perceives the sublime importance of it, as a regulator of human intercourse, could find a motive to misrepresent it. Education, drill, on this great theme, seem to be indispensable.

481. A volume wholly devoted to its illustration as *the* great Divine law of order and as a preventive of confusion and violence, could scarcely begin to do it justice, and all that can be done here is to excite thought towards it as a study, by a few hints, in addition to those already given, and leave it to

the after-experience of the reader for continuous illustration and confirmation. . . .

511. Had the American public mind been educated to understand that *Individuality* is the vital principle of order, it would have generally seen and admitted that Government has, properly, but one (*Individual*) function, which is to resist or restrain encroachments upon the rights of Individuals. That it is not the true function of governments to prescribe opinions, either moral, religious, or political; to meddle with manufactures or importations; to prescribe the cut of the citizen's hair, the employment of his time, or the disposal of his life or his property, *but simply and solely to protect him against such impertinences.* . . .

520. How is it, then, with Individuality? Is it the great element of discord, of *divergence,* of selfishness, isolation, and antagonism, or is it the great element of order, peace, reconciliation, convergency, co-operation, and prosperity?

521. A commentator has well said, "*Individuality* is the next thing to everything;" and but little justice can be done to it within the limits now at command.

522. The study of it, instead of being, as it should be, the first step in the foundation of Education, it remains yet to be taken!

523. Education will not fairly have commenced until each child has its own little *Individual* sphere of personality, property, of time and responsibilities, over which he or she has supreme or sovereign control, disintegrated from the control of its parents (except as counsellors), who, by a watchful regard to its legitimate sovereignty within its own little sphere, teaches it, by example, to respect the same rights in its parents and all others. It is only within these conditions

that the child begins to be prepared for successful future life....

556. The only possible apparent solution or settlement of this vital subject is in LIMITING THE SPHERE WITHIN WHICH EACH INDIVIDUAL CAN HARMLESSLY BE SOVEREIGN OR ABSOLUTELY FREE, ACCORDING TO HIS OWN INTERPRETATION OF THAT WORD, or any other word.

557. This sphere includes at least his *own person, his own time, his own property, and his own responsibilities....*

559. INDIVIDUALITY is the great corner-stone of order.

560. SELF-SOVEREIGNTY is the mandate of peace.

17. FROM *THE NATURAL AND ARTIFICIAL RIGHT OF PROPERTY CONTRASTED*

THOMAS HODGSKIN

The Natural and Artificial Right of Property Contrasted (London: B. Steil, Paternoster Row, 1832)

The Englishman Thomas Hodgskin (1787–1869) was one of the best libertarian theoreticians of the 19th century. Although not as well known as his younger contemporary Herbert Spencer, Hodgskin's approach to libertarianism was more consistent. Hodgskin's books include Travels in the North of Germany *(in two volumes) and* Popular Political Economy. *His best known if least satisfactory work,* Labour Defended Against the Claims of Capital, *has led to a common misconception that Hodgskin was a socialist, whereas he was, in fact an individualist libertarian who staunchly defended laissez-faire and the rights of private property. In our excerpt from* The Natural and Artificial Right of Property Contrasted, *his greatest work, Hodgskin builds from Lockean premises to the conclusion that our sense of property is inextricably linked to our sense of individuality.*

Allow me . . . at once to declare (as there have been in almost every age individuals, such as Beccaria and Rousseau—and sects, some existing at present, such as Mr. Owen's cooperative societies, the Saint Simonians in France, and the Moravians, who have asserted that all the evils of society arise from *a* right of property, the utility of which they have accordingly and utterly denied) allow me to separate myself entirely from them, by declaring that

I look on *a right* of property—on the right of individuals, to have and to own, for their own separate and selfish use and enjoyment, the produce of their own industry, with power freely to dispose of the whole of that in the manner most agreeable to themselves, as essential to the welfare and even to the continued existence of society. If, therefore, I did not suppose, with Mr. Locke, that nature establishes such a right—if I were not prepared to show that she not merely establishes, but also protects and preserves it, so far as never to suffer it to be violated with impunity—I should at once take refuge in Mr. Bentham's impious theory, and admit that the legislator who established and preserved a right of property, deserved little less adoration than the Divinity himself. Believing, however, that nature establishes such a right, I can neither join those who vituperate it as the source of all our social misery, nor those who claim for the legislator the high honour of being "the author of the finest triumph of humanity over itself."

I heartily and cordially concur with Mr. Locke, in his view of the origin and foundation of a right of property. "Every man," he says, "has a property in his own person that nobody has any right to but himself. The labour of his body and the work of his hand are his property. Whatsoever, then, he removes out of the state that nature hath provided and left it in, he hath mixed his labour with it and joined to something that is his own, and thereby makes it his property. It being by him removed from the common state nature hath placed it in, it hath by this labour something annexed to it that excludes the common right of other men. *For the labour being the unquestionable property of the labourer, no man but he can have a right to what that is joined to*—at least, where there is enough and as good left in common for others." ...

Thus the principle Mr. Locke lays down is, that nature gives to each individual his body and his labour; and what he can make or obtain by his labour naturally belongs to him. Though I cannot make this principle any clearer by repeating the statement in my own way, yet as different minds are affected by different means, the object I have in view may, perhaps, be promoted, by putting it in a somewhat different, even if it be not so clear a form. The power to labour is the gift of nature to each individual; and the power which belongs to each, cannot be confounded with that which belongs to another: The natural wants of man, particularly of food and clothing, are the natural stimulus to exert this power; and the means of gratifying them, which it provides, is the natural reward of the exertion. The power to labour and the natural wants which stimulate labour, are generally found together; thus we see that the motive to labour—the power to labour—and the produce of labour—all exist exclusive of all legislation.

Nature, not the legislator, creates man with these wants, and conjoins with them the power to gratify them. The unpleasant feeling of hunger may be properly called a command or admonition to labour. Nature gives also to each individual: and her separate gifts—as, for example, the fish she bestows on him who baits a hook and watches the line—can no more be confounded with those she gives to another, than the distinct and separate wants they are intended to gratify. The commodities which labour, acting in obedience to this command, creates or obtains, nature—or God, (for it is better to use the latter term than the former)—bestows on labour; and He gives to labour, if violence and wrong interfere not, whatever it can make. On the naked savage, and on him alone, the Almighty primarily bestows the wild fruits he gathers, and the game he kills; to him, exclusively, the Creator gives the branch he rends from the parent stem, and confirms it in his possession, while he fashions it into a club, by the stone hatchet he has previously made, and therefore calls his: as well as guarantees its use to him by the wish and power He continually engenders to retain and use it. A savage, stronger than the labourer or more cunning, may undoubtedly take the fruit of his industry from him by force or fraud; but antecedently to the use of force or fraud, and antecedently to all legislation, nature bestows on every individual what his labour produces, just as she gives him his own body. She bestows the wish and the power to produce, she couples them with the expectation of enjoying that which is produced, and she confirms in the labourer's possession, if no wrong be practised, as long as he wishes to possess, whatever he makes or produces. All these are natural circumstances—the existence of any other person than the labourer not being necessary to the full accomplishment of them. The enjoyment is secured by the individual's own means. No contract, no legislation, is required. Whatever is made by human industry, is naturally appropriated as made, and belongs to the maker. In substance, I would feign hope, there is no difference between this statement and that of Mr. Locke; but I wish to mark, stronger than I think he has done, the fact, that, antecedently to all legislation, and to any possible interference by the legislator, nature establishes a law of appropriation by bestowing, as she creates individuality, the produce of labour on the labourer.

Mr. Locke says, that every man has a property in his own person; in fact, individuality—which is signified by the word *own*—cannot be disjoined from the person. Each individual learns his own shape and form, and even the existence of his limbs and body, from seeing and feeling them. These constitute his notion of *personal* identity, both for himself and others; and it is impossible to conceive—it is in fact a contradiction to say—that a man's limbs and body do not belong to himself: for the words him, self, and his body, signify the same material thing.

As we learn the existence of our own bodies from seeing and feeling them, and as we see and feel the bodies of others, we have precisely similar grounds for believing in the individuality or identity of other persons, as for believing in our own identity. The ideas expressed by the words mine and thine, as applied to the produce of labour, are simply then an extended form of the ideas of personal identity and individuality. We readily spread them from our hands and other limbs, to the things the hands seize, or fashion, or create, or the legs hunt down and overtake. Nor is this extension limited to material objects. Were it not the practice to despise the sententious wisdom of proverbs, I might quote several: such as this—"As you make your bed, so you must lie in it"—to show that these ideas are generally extended to the immaterial consequences of our actions. In the popular creed, the pleasure or pain that results from an individual's conduct, his hopes or his despair, his remorse or his self approbation, are properly deemed to belong to him, equally with the book he writes or the game he kills. In fact, the material objects are only sought after for the immaterial pleasure they bestow.

By the operations of nature, then, it being, indeed, the necessary consequence of existence, there arises in every individual, unwilled by any lawgiver, a distinct notion of his own individuality and of the individuality of others. By the same operations, we extend this idea, first for ourselves and afterwards for others, to the things we make or create, or have given to us, including the pleasure or pain resulting from our own conduct. Thus, the natural idea of property is a mere extension of that of individuality; and it embraces all the mental as well as all the physical consequences of muscular exertion. As nature gives to labour whatever it produces—as we extend the idea of personal individuality to what is produced by every individual—not merely is a right of property established by nature, we see also that she takes means to make known the existence of that right. It is as impossible for men not to have a notion of a right of property, as it is for them to want the idea of personal identity. When either is totally absent man is insane.

PART FOUR

POLITICAL INDIVIDUALISM

---

18. FROM *THE RELIGION OF NATURE DELINEATED*

WILLIAM WOLLASTON

The Religion of Nature Delineated, 7th ed. (London: J. and P. Knapton, 1750), 234–269

[Spelling and punctuation have been modernized, and most italics have been omitted. Wollaston's footnotes, which cite various classical sources, are not included.]

---

*Educated at Cambridge, William Wollaston (1660–1724) took holy orders in the Anglican Church and, after attaining financial security through an inheritance, devoted his life to scholarly pursuits. Although Wollaston wrote a fair amount, he published very little—*The Religion of Nature Delineated *being his only major work. This book sold well, going through eight editions by 1750 and selling more than 10,000 copies. The last edition appeared in 1759, and the work was not reprinted until 1974. During this gap of more than 200 years, Wollaston's moral theory, as one commentator noted, "was soon relegated to the curiosity section of the philosophical museum."*

Most philosophers who did not ignore Wollaston ridiculed him instead. David Hume made him the butt of a joke, and Wollaston fared little better at the hands of Jeremy Bentham. The English historian Leslie Stephen, after misrepresenting Wollaston, concluded that he "inevitably fails to extract any intelligible result from [his] fanciful form of an illusory theory."

Some commentators have been kinder to Wollaston. The great freethought scholar J. M. Robertson characterized him as a "vivid,

*interesting, thoughtful, and very learned writer"; Ernest Mossner (a biog-
rapher of David Hume) called him "a man of vast erudition." More recently (1977), Stanley Tweyman claimed that "the available literature
has not offered effective criticisms against his views, nor has it been shown
that Wollaston's book is without lasting significance." And philosopher Joel
Feinberg corrected some common distortions of Wollaston's ideas.*

*Friend and foe alike, however, have focused on Wollaston's ethical theory
while neglecting his theory of property, which is based on the unique individuality of each human being. The following excerpt deals with that topic.*

I. *Every man has in himself a principle of individuation which distinguishes
and separates him from all other men in such a manner as may render him
and them capable of distinct properties in things (or distinct subjects of property).* That is, B and C are so distinguished, or exist so distinctly, that
if there be anything which B can call his, it will be for that reason
not C's: and . . . what is C's will for that reason not be B's. . . .

II. *There are some things to which (at least before the case is altered by
voluntary subjection, compact, or the like) every individual man has, or
may have, such a natural and immediate relation that he only of all
mankind can call them his.*

The life, limbs, etc., of B are as much his as B is himself. It is impossible for C or any other to see with the eyes of B. Therefore
they are eyes only to B, and when they cease to be his eyes, they
cease to be eyes at all. He then has the sole property in them, it
being impossible in nature that the eyes of B should ever be the
eyes of C.

Further, the labor of B cannot be the labor of C, because it is
the application of the organs and powers of B, not of C, to the
effecting of something; and therefore the labor is as much B's as
the limbs and faculties made use of are his.

Again, the effect or produce of the labor of B is not the effect of the labor of C; and therefore this effect or produce is B's, not C's—as much B's as the labor was B's and not C's. Because what the labor of B causes or produces, B produces by his labor, or it is the product of B by his labor; that is, it is B's product, not C's or any other's. And if C should pretend to any property in that which B only can truly call his, he would act contrary to truth. . . .

IV. *Whatever is either reasonable or unreasonable in B with respect to C would be just the same in C with respect to B if the case was inverted.* Because reason is universal and respects cases, not persons.

Hence it follows that a good way to know what is right or wrong in relation to other men is to consider what we should take things to be were we in their circumstances.

V. *In a state of nature men are equal in respect of dominion.* I except for the present the case of parents and their children, and perhaps of some few other near relations. Here let me be understood to mean only those between whom there is no family relation (or between whom all family relation is vanished).

In a state where no laws of society make any subordination or distinction, men can only be considered as men, or only as individuals of the same species, and equally sharing in one common definition. And since by virtue of this same definition B is the same to C that C is to B, B has no more dominion over C than C reciprocally has over B; that is, they are in this regard equal.

Personal excellences or defects can make no difference here, because:

1. Who must judge on which side the advantage lies? To say B (or D, or anybody else) has a right to judge to the disadvantage of C is to suppose what is in question, a dominion over him, not to prove it.

2. Great natural or acquired endowments may be privileges to them who have them, but this does not deprive those who have less of their title to what they have; or, which is the same, give any one who has greater abilities a right to take it or the use of it from them. If B has better eyes than C, it is well for him, but it does not follow from this that C should not therefore see for himself and use his eyes as freely as B may his. C's eyes are accommodated by nature to his use, and so are B's to his, and each has the sole property in his own, so their respective properties are equal. The case would be parallel to this if B should happen to have better intellectual faculties than C. And, further, if B should be stronger than C, he would not yet for that reason have any right to be his lord. For C's less degree of strength is as much his as B's greater is his. Therefore C has as much right to his, and (which is the natural consequence) to use his as B has to use his; that is, C has as much right to resist as B has to impose or command by virtue of his strength. And where the right (though not the power) of resisting is equal to the right of commanding, the right of commanding or dominion is nothing.

3. Since strength and power are most apt to pretend a title to dominion, it may be added further that power and right, or a power of doing anything and right to do it, are quite different ideas, and therefore they may be separated. Nor does one [imply] the other. Lastly, if power qua power gives a right to dominion, it gives a right to everything that is obnoxious to it, and then nothing can be done that is wrong. (For nobody can do anything which he has not the power to do.) [B]ut to assert [this] would be to advance a plain absurdity or contradiction rather. For then to oppose the man who has this power as far as one can, or (which is the same)

as far as one has the power to do it, would not be wrong; and yet so it must be if he has a right to dominion or to be not opposed. Moreover, that a man should have a right to anything merely because he has the power to take it is a doctrine indeed which may serve a few tyrants, or some banditti and rogues, but directly opposite to the peace and general good of mankind.... It is also what the powerful themselves could not allow if they would but imagine themselves to be in the state of the weak and more defenseless....

VI. *No man can have a right to begin to interrupt the happiness of another.* Because, in the first place, this supposes a dominion over him, and the most absolute too that can be. In the next, for B to begin to disturb the peace and happiness of C is what B would think unreasonable if he was in C's case. In the last, since it is supposed that C has never invaded the happiness of B, nor taken anything from him, nor at all meddled with him, but the whole transaction begins originally from B (for all this is couched in the word begin), C can have nothing that is B's and therefore nothing to which C has not at least as good a title as B has; or, in other words, nothing which C has not as much right to keep as B to claim. These two rights being then at least equal and counterpoising each other, no alteration in the present state of things can follow from any superiority of right in B, and therefore it must of right remain as it is; and what C has must, for any right that B has to oppose this settlement, remain with C in his undisturbed possession. But the argument is still stronger on the side of C, because he seems to have such a property in his own happiness [that] no other can have.

[*Inserted from a previous section.* Men's respective happinesses or pleasures ought to be valued as they are to the persons themselves, whose they are, or according to the thoughts and sense which they have of them; not according to the estimate put upon them by other people, who have no authority to judge of them, nor can know what they are, may compute by different rules, have less sense, be in different circumstances, or such as guilt has rendered partial to themselves. . . . Every man's happiness is his happiness, what it is to him; and the loss of it is answerable to the degrees of his perception, to his manner of taking things, to his wants and circumstances.]

VII. *Though no man can have a right to begin to interrupt another man's happiness or to hurt him, yet every man has a right to defend himself and his against violence, to recover what is taken by force from him, and even to make reprisals by all the means that truth and prudence permit.* . . .

Great part of the general happiness of mankind depends upon those means by which the innocent may be saved from their cruel invaders, among which the opportunities they have of defending themselves may be reckoned the chief. Therefore to debar men of the use of these opportunities, and the right of defending themselves against injurious treatment and violence, must be inconsistent with the laws of nature.

If a man has no right to defend himself and what is his, he can have no right to anything . . . since that cannot be his right which he may not maintain to be his right. . . . He who begins is the true cause of all that follows, and whatever falls upon him from the opposition made by the defending party is but the effect of his own act. [I]t is that violence, of which he is the author, reflected back upon himself. It is as when a man spits at heaven, and the spittle falls back upon his own face. . . .

Lastly, since every man is obliged to consult his own happiness, there can be no doubt but that he not only may but even ought to defend it, in such a manner, I mean, as does not interfere with truth or his own design of being happy. He ought indeed not to act rashly or do more than the end proposed requires. That is, he ought by a prudent carriage and wise forecast to shut up, if he can, the avenues by which he may be invaded; and when that cannot be done, to use arguments and [persuasion], or perhaps withdraw out of the way of harm. But when these measures are ineffectual or impracticable, he must take such other as he can, and confront force with force. . . .

By the same means that a man may defend what is his, he may certainly endeavor to recover what has been by any kind of violence or villainy taken from him. For it has been shown already that the power to take anything from another gives no right to it. The right then to that which has been taken from its owner against his will remains still where it was. He may still truly call it his; and if it be his, he may use it as his, which if he who took it away, or any other, shall hinder him from doing, that man is even here the aggressor, and the owner does but defend himself and what is his. . . .

Then, further, if a man hath still a right to what is forcibly or without his consent taken from him, he must have a right to the value of it. For the thing is to him what it is in value to him, and the right he has to it may be considered as a right to a thing of such a value. So that if the very thing which was taken be destroyed or cannot be retrieved, the proprietor nevertheless retains his right to a thing of such a value to him, and something must be had in lieu of it; that is, he has a right to make reprisals. Since every thing is to every man what it is in value to him, things of the same value to any one may be reckoned as to him the same, and to recover the equivalent [is] the same as to recover the thing itself, for otherwise it is not an equivalent. If the thing taken by way of reprisal should be to the man from whom it is taken of greater value than what he wrongfully took from the recoverer, he must charge himself with that loss. If injustice be done him, it is done by himself. . . . To which add, that as a man has a right to recover what is his or the equivalent from an invader, so he seems for the same reasons to have a right to an equivalent for the expense he is at in recovering his own, for the loss of time and quiet, and for the trouble, hazards, and dangers undergone; because all these are the effects of the invasion and therefore to be added to the invader's account. . . .

IX. *A title to many things may be transferred by compact or donation.* If B has the sole right in lands or goods, nobody has any right to the disposal of them besides B, and he has a right. For disposing of them is but using them as his. Therefore the act of B in exchanging them for something else, or bestowing them upon C, interferes not with truth, and so B does nothing that is wrong. Nor does C do anything against truth or that is wrong in taking them, because he treats them as being what they are: as things which come to him by the act of that person in whom is lodged the sole power of disposing of them. Thus C gets the title innocently.

But in the case of compact the reason on which this transaction stands is more evident still. For the contractors are supposed to receive each from other the equivalent of that which they part with, or at least what is equivalent to them respectively, or perhaps by each party preferable. Thus neither of them is hurt, perhaps both advantaged. And so each of them treats the thing which he receives upon the innocent exchange as being what it is: better for him, and promoting his convenience and happiness. Indeed he who receives the value of anything, and what he likes as well, in effect has it still. His property is not diminished; the situation and matter of it is only altered.

Mankind could not well subsist without bartering one thing for another. Therefore whatever tends to take away the benefit of this intercourse is inconsistent with the general good of mankind. If a man could find the necessaries of life without it and by himself, he must at least want many of the comforts of it.

X. *There is then such a thing as property founded in nature and truth; or, there are things which one man only can consistently with nature and truth call his.*

XI. *Those things which only one man can truly and properly call his must remain his until he agrees to part with them (if they are such as he may part with) by compact or donation*; or (which must be understood) till they fail or death extinguishes him and his title together, and he delivers the lamp to his next man. . . .

XII. *To have the property of any thing and to have the sole right of using and disposing of it are the same thing; they are equipollent expressions.* For when it is said that P has the property, or that such a thing is proper to P, it is not said that P and Q or P and others have the property (*proprium* limits the thing to P only); and when any thing is said to be his, it is not said that part of it only is his. P has therefore the all or all-hood of it, and consequently all the use of it. And, then, since the all of it to him, or all that P can have of it, is but the use and disposal of it, he who has this has the thing itself, and it is his. . . .

XIV. *To usurp or invade the property of another man is injustice. Or, more fully, to take, detain, use, destroy, hurt, or meddle with anything that is his without his allowance, either by force or fraud or any other way, or even to attempt any of these or assist them who do, are acts of injustice. The contrary, to render and permit quietly to everyone what is his, is justice.*

19. FROM *LETTERS TO CATHERINE E. BEECHER*

ANGELINA E. GRIMKE

Letters to Catherine E. Beecher, in Reply to An Essay on Slavery and Abolitionism (Boston: Isaac Knapp, 1838)

Angelina Grimke (1805–79), like her sister Sarah Grimke, was a prominent abolitionist and an early crusader for women's rights. This excerpt from one of her abolitionist tracts shows the crucial role that the individualist principle of self-ownership played in the antislavery movement.

The great fundamental principle of Abolitionists is, that man cannot rightfully hold his fellow man as property. Therefore, we affirm, that *every slaveholder is a man-stealer*. We do so, for the following reasons: to steal a man is to rob him of himself. It matters not whether this be done in Guinea, or Carolina; a man is a *man,* and *as* a man he has *inalienable* rights, among which is the right to personal *liberty*. Now if every man has an *inalienable* right to personal liberty, it follows, that he cannot rightfully be reduced to slavery. But I find in these United States, 2,250,000 men, women and children, robbed of that to which they have an *inalienable* right. How comes this to pass? Where millions are plundered, are there no *plunderers?* If, then, the slaves have been robbed of their liberty, *who* has robbed them? Not the man who stole their forefathers from Africa, but he who now holds them in bondage; no matter *how* they came into his possession, whether he inherited them, or bought them, or seized them at their birth on his own plantation. The only difference I can see between the original man-stealer, who caught the African in his native country, and the American slaveholder, is, that the former committed *one* act of robbery, while the other perpetrates the same crime *continually*. Slaveholding is the perpetrating of acts, all of the same kind, in a *series*, the first of which is technically called man-stealing. The *first* act robbed the man of himself; and the same state of mind that prompted *that act, keeps up the series*, having *taken* his all from him: it *keeps* his all from him, not only *refusing* to *restore*, but still robbing him of all he gets, and as fast as he gets it. Slaveholding, then, is *the constant or habitual perpetration of the act of man-stealing. To make* a slave is *man-stealing—the* ACT *itself—*to *hold* him such is man-stealing—the *habit*, the *permanent* state, made up of *individual* acts. In other words—to *begin* to hold a slave is man-stealing—to *keep on* holding him is merely a *repetition* of the first act—a doing of the same identical thing *all the time*. A series of the same acts continued for a length of time is a *habit—a permanent state*. And the *first* of this series of the *same* acts that make up this *habit* or state is just like all the rest.

If every slave has a right to freedom, then surely the man who withholds that right from him to-day is a man-stealer, though he may not be the first person who has robbed him of it. Hence we find that Wesley says—'Men-*buyers* are *exactly on a level* with men-*stealers.*' And again—'Much less is it possible that any child of man should ever be *born a slave.*' Hear also Jonathan Edwards—'To hold a man in a state of slavery, is to be *every day guilty* of robbing him of his liberty, or of *man-stealing.*' And Grotius says—'Those are men-stealers who abduct, *keep*, sell or buy *slaves* or freemen.'

If thou meanest merely that *acts* of that *same nature*, but differently located in a series, are designated by different terms, thus pointing out their different *relative positions*, then thy argument concedes what we affirm,—the identity in the *nature* of the acts, and thus it dwindles to a mere philological criticism, or rather a mere play upon words.

20. FROM *THE VOLUNTARYIST CREED*

AUBERON HERBERT

The Voluntaryist Creed: Being the Herbert Spencer Lecture Delivered at Oxford, June 7, 1906 (London: Oxford University, 1908)

Auberon Herbert (1838–1906) studied at Oxford and served in the British army. Herbert was a member of Parliament from 1870 to 1874, only to repudiate, under the influence of Herbert Spencer, the political process as a means of bringing about social change. Herbert turned instead to individualism and the spontaneous, voluntary cooperation of free individuals in a free market. In the following excerpt from The Voluntaryist Creed, *Herbert contrasts a society governed by political power with a society of free individuals.*

We, who call ourselves Voluntaryists, appeal to you to free yourselves from these many systems of State force, which are rendering impossible the true and the happy life of the nations of today. This ceaseless effort to compel each other, in turn for each new object that is clamored for by this or that set of politicians, this ceaseless effort to bind chains round the hands of each other, is preventing progress of the real kind, is preventing peace and friendship and brotherhood, and is turning the men of the same nation, who ought to labor happily together for common ends, in their own groups, in their own free unfettered fashion, into enemies, who live conspiring against and dreading, often hating each other. . . .

. . . What good, what happiness, what permanent progress of the true kind can come out of that unnatural, denationalizing, miserable warfare? Why should you desire to compel others; why should you seek to have power—that evil, bitter, mocking thing, which has been from of old, as it is today, the sorrow and curse of the world—over your fellow men and fellow women? Why should you desire to take from any man or woman their own will and intelligence, their free choice, their own self-guidance, their inalienable rights over themselves; why should you desire to make of them mere tools and instruments for your own advantage and interest; why should you desire to compel them to serve and follow your opinions instead of their own; why should you deny in them the soul—that suffers so deeply from all constraint—and treat them as a sheet of blank paper upon which you may write your own will and desires, of whatever kind they may happen to be? Who gave you the right, from where do you pretend to have received it, to degrade other men and women from their own true rank as human beings, taking from them their will, their conscience, and intelligence—in a word, all the best and highest part of their nature—turning them into mere empty worthless shells, mere shadows of the true man and woman, mere counters in the game you are mad enough to play; and just because you are more numerous or stronger than they, to treat them as if they belonged not to themselves, but to you? Can you believe that good will ever come by morally and spiritually degrading your fellow men? What happy and safe and permanent form of society can you hope to build on this pitiful plan of subjecting others, or being yourselves subjected by them?

We show you the better way. We ask you to renounce this old, weary, hopeless way of force, ever tear-stained and blood-stained, which has gone on so long under Emperors and autocrats and governing classes, and still goes on to-day amongst those who, whilst they condemn Emperors and autocrats, continue to walk in their footsteps, and understand and love liberty very little more than those old rulers of an old world. We bid you ask yourselves—'What is all our boasted civilization and gain in knowledge worth to us, if we are still, like those who had not attained to our civilization and knowledge, to hunger for power, still to cling to the ways of strife and bitterness and hatred, still to oppress each other as in the days of the old rulers?' Don't be deceived by mere words and phrases. Don't think that everything was gained when you got rid of autocrat and emperor. Don't think that a change in the mere form—without change in the spirit of men—can really alter anything, or make a new world. A voting majority, that still believes in force, that still believes in crushing and ruling a minority, can be just as tyrannous, as selfish and blind, as any of the old rulers. . . .

And are the conquerors in the great conflict better off—if we try to see clearly—than the conquered? We can only answer—No; for power is one of the worst, the most fatal and demoralizing of all gifts you can place in the hands of men. He who has power—power only limited by his own desires—misunderstands both himself and the world in which he lives; . . . If you wish to know how power spoils character and narrows intelligence, look at the great military empires; their steady perseverance in the roads that lead to ruin; their dread of free thought and of liberty in all its forms; look at the sharp repressions, the excessive punishments, the love of secrecy, the attempt to drill a whole nation into obedience, and to use the drilled and subject thing for every passing vanity and aggrandizement of those who govern. Look also at the great administrative systems. See how men become under them helpless and dispirited, incapable of free effort and self-protection, at one moment sunk in apathy, at another moment ready for revolution. Do you wonder that it is so? Is it wonderful that when you replace the will and intelligence and self-guidance of the individual by systems of vast machinery, that men should gradually lose all the better and higher parts of their nature—for of what use to them is that better and higher part, when they may not exercise it?. . .

. . .And thus it is that seeking for power not only means strife and hatred, the splitting of a nation into hostile factions, but for ever breeds trick and intrigue and falsehood, results in the wholesale buying of men, the offering of this or that unworthy bribe, the playing with passions, the poor unworthy trade of the bitter unscrupulous tongue, that heaps every kind of abuse, deserved or not deserved, upon those who are opposed to you, that exaggerates their every fault, mistake, and weakness, that caricatures, perverts their words and actions, and claims in childish and absurd fashion that what is good is only to be found in your half of the nation, and what is evil is only to be found in the other half. . . .

Such are the fruits of the strife for power. Evil they must be, because power is evil in itself. How can the taking away from a man his intelligence, his will, his self-guidance be anything but evil? If it were not evil in itself, there would be no meaning in the higher part of nature, there would be no guidance in the great principles—for power, if we once acknowledge it, must stand above everything else, and cannot admit of any rivals. If the power of some and the subjection of others are right, then men would exist merely as the dust to be trodden under the feet of each other; the autocrats, the emperors, the military empires, the Socialist, perhaps even the Anarchist with his detestable bomb, would each and all be in their own right, and find their own justification; and we should live in a world of perpetual warfare, that some devil, as we might reasonably believe, must have planned for us. To those of us who believe in the soul—and on that great matter we who sign hold different opinions—the freedom of the individual is not simply a question of politics, but it is a religious question of the deepest meaning. The soul to us is by its own nature a free thing, living its life here in order that it may learn to distinguish and choose between the good and the evil, to find its own way—whatever stages of existence may have to be passed through—towards the perfecting of itself. You may not then, either for the sake of advancing your own interests, or for the sake of helping any cause, however great and desirable in itself, in which you believe, place bonds on the souls of other men and women, and take from them any part of their freedom. You may not take away the free life, putting in its place the bound life. Religion that is not based on freedom, that allows any form of servitude of men to men, is to us only an empty and mocking word, for religion means following our own personal sense of right and fulfilling the commands of duty, as we each can most truly read it, not with the hands tied and the eyes blinded, but with the free, unconstrained heart that chooses for itself. And see clearly that you cannot divide men up into separate parts—into social, political and religious beings. It is all one. All parts of our nature are joined in one great unity; and you cannot therefore make men politically subject without injuring their souls. Those who strive to increase the power of men over men, and who thus create the habit of mechanical obedience, turning men into mere State creatures, over whose heads laws of all kinds are passed, are striking at the very roots of religion, which becomes but a lifeless, meaningless thing, sinking gradually into a matter of forms and ceremonies, whenever the soul loses its freedom. Many men recognize this truth, if not in words, yet in their hearts, for all religions of the higher kind tend to become intensely personal, resting upon that free spiritual relation with the great Over-soul—a relation that each must interpret for himself. And remember you can't have two opposed powers of equal authority; you can't serve two masters. Either the religious conscience and sense of right must stand in the first place, and the commands of all governing authorities in the second place; or the State machine must stand first, and the religious and moral conscience of men must follow after in humble subjection, and do what the State orders. If you make the State supreme, why should it pay heed to the rule of conscience, or the individual sense of right; why should the master listen to the servant? If it is supreme, let it plainly say so, take its own way, and pay no heed, as so many rulers before them have refused to do, to the conscience of those they rule. . . .

Such are the fruits of power and the strife for power. It must be so. Set men up to rule their fellow men, to treat them as mere soulless material with which they may deal as they please, and the consequence is that you sweep away every moral landmark and turn this world into a place of selfish striving, hopeless confusion, trickery and violence, a mere scrambling-ground for the strongest or the most cunning or the most numerous. Once more we repeat—don't be deluded by the careless everyday talk about majorities. The vote of a majority is a far lesser evil than the edict of an autocrat, for you can appeal to a majority to repent of its sins and to undo its mistakes, but numbers—though they were as the grains of sand on the seashore—cannot take away the rights of a single individual, cannot turn man or woman into stuff for the politician to play with, or over-rule the great principles which mark out our relations to each other. These principles are rooted in the very nature of our being, and have nothing to do with minorities and majorities. Arithmetic is a very excellent thing in its place, but it can neither give nor take away rights. Because you can collect three men on one side, and only two on the other side, that can offer no reason—no shadow of a reason—why the three men should dispose of the lives and property of the two men, should settle for them what they are to do, and what they are to be: that mere rule of numbers can never justify the turning of the two men into slaves, and the three men into slaveowners. There is one and only one principle, on which you can build a true, rightful, enduring and progressive civilization, which can give peace and friendliness and contentment to all differing groups and sects into which we are divided—and that principle is that every man and woman should be held by us all sacredly and religiously to be the one true owner of his or her faculties, of his or her body and mind, and of all property, inherited or—honestly acquired. There is no other possible foundation—seek it wherever you will— on which you can build, if you honestly mean to make this world a place of peace and friendship, where progress of every kind, like a full river fed by its many streams, may flow on its happy fertilizing course, with ever broadening and deepening volume.

We ask you then to limit and restrain power, as you would restrain a wild and dangerous beast. Make everything subservient to liberty; use State force only for one purpose—to prevent and restrain the use of force amongst ourselves, and that which may be described as the twin-brother of force, wearing a mask over its features, the fraud, which by cunning sets aside the consent of the individual, as force sets it aside openly and violently. Restrain by simple and efficient machinery the force and fraud that some men are always ready to employ against other men, for whether it is the State that employs force against a part of the citizens, or one citizen who employs force or fraud against another citizen, in both cases it is equally an aggression upon the rights, upon the self-ownership of the individual; it is equally in both cases the act of the stronger who in virtue of his strength preys upon the weaker....

...Has not the real prosperity, the happiness, the peace of a nation increased just in proportion as it has broken all the bonds and disabilities that impeded its life, just in proportion as it has let liberty replace force; just in proportion as it has chosen and established for itself all rights of opinion, of meeting, of discussion, rights of free trade, rights of the free use of faculties, rights of self-ownership as against the wrongs of subjection? And do you think that these new bonds and restrictions in which the nations of to-day have allowed themselves to be entangled—the conscription which sends men out to fight, consenting or not consenting, which treats them as any other war-material, as the guns and the rifles dispatched in batches to do their work; or the great systems of taxation, which make of the individual mere tax-material, as conscription makes of him mere war-material; or the great systems of compulsory education, under which the State on its own unavowed interest tries to exert more and more of its own influence and authority over the minds of the children, tries—as we see specially in other countries—to mould and to shape those young minds for its own ends—Something of religion will be useful—school-made patriotism will be useful—drilling will be useful—so preparing from the start docile and obedient State-material, ready made for taxation, ready made for conscription—ready made for the ambitious aims and ends of the rulers—do you think that any of these modern systems, though they are more veiled, more subtle, less frank and brutal than the systems of the older governments, though the poison in them is more thickly smeared with the coating of sugar, will bear different fruit, will work less evil amongst us all, will endure longer than those other broken and discredited attempts, which men again and again in their madness and presumption have made to possess themselves of and to rule the bodies and minds of others? No! one and all they belong to the same evil family; they are all part of the same conspiracy against the true greatness of human nature; they are all marked broad across the forehead with the same old curse; and they will all end in the same shameful and sorrowful ending. Over us all is the great unchanging law, ever the same, unchanged and unchanging, regardless of all our follies and delusions, that come and go, that we are not to take possession of and rule the body and mind of others; that we are not to take away from our fellow-beings their own intelligence, their own choice, their own conscience and free will; that we are not to allow any ruler, be it autocrat, emperor, parliament, or voting crowd, to take from any human being his own true rank, making of him the degraded State-material that others use for their own purposes. . . .

. . .Force—whatever forms it takes—can do nothing for you. It can redeem nothing; it can give you nothing that is worth the having, nothing that will endure; it cannot even give you material prosperity. There is no salvation for you or for any living man to be won by the force that narrows rights, and always leaves men lower and more brutal in character than it found them. It is, and ever has been the evil genius of our race. It calls out the reckless, violent, cruel part of our nature, it wastes precious human effort in setting men to strive one against the other; it turns us into mere fighting animals; and ends, when men at last become sick of the useless strife and universal confusion, in 'the man on the black horse' who calls himself and is greeted as 'the saviour of society'. Make the truer, the nobler choice. Resist the blind and sordid appeal to your interests of the moment, and take your place once and for good on the side of the true liberty, that calls out all the better and higher part of our nature, and knows no difference between rulers and ruled, majorities and minorities, rich and poor. Declare once and for good that all men and women are the only true owners of their faculties, of their mind and body, of the property that belongs to them; that you will only build the new society on the one true foundation of self-ownership, self-rule, and self-guidance; that you turn away from and renounce utterly all this mischievous, foolish and corrupt business of compelling each other, of placing burdens upon each other, of making force, and the hateful trickery that always goes with it, into our guiding principles, of treating first one set of men and then another set of men as beasts of burden, whose lot in life it is to serve the purposes of others. True it is that there are many and many things good in themselves which you do not yet possess, and which you rightly desire, things which the believers in force are generous enough to offer you in any profusion at the expense of others; but they are merely cheating you with vain hopes, dangling before your eyes the mocking shows of things that can never be. Force never yet made a nation prosperous. It has destroyed nation after nation, but never yet built up an enduring prosperity. It is through your own free efforts, not through the gifts of those who have no right to give them, that all these good things can come to you; for great is the essential difference between the gift— whether rightly or wrongly given—and the thing won by free effort. That which you have won has made you stronger in yourselves, has taught you to know your own power and resources, has prepared you to win more and more victories. The gift flung to you has left you dependent upon others, distrustful and dispirited in yourselves. Why turn to your governments as if you were helpless in yourselves? What power lies in a government, that does not lie also in you?. . . You have in yourselves the great qualities—though still undeveloped—for supplying in your own free groups the growing wants of your lives. You are the children of the men who did so much for themselves, the men who broke the absolute power; who planted the colonies of our race in distant lands, who created our manufactures, and carried our trade to every part of the world; who established your co-operative and benefit societies, your Trade Unions, who built and supported your Nonconformist Churches. In you is the same stuff, the same power to do, as there was in them; and if only you let their spirit breathe again in you, and tread in their footsteps, you may add to their triumphs and successes tenfold and a hundredfold. . . .

But nothing can be well and rightly done, nothing can bear the true fruit, until you become deeply and devotedly in love with personal liberty, consecrating in your hearts the great and sacred principle of self-ownership and self-direction. That great principle must be our guiding star through the whole of this life's pilgrimage. Away from its guiding we shall only continue to wander, as of old, hopelessly in the wilderness. For its sake we must be ready to make any and every sacrifice. It is worth them all—many times worth them all. For its sake you must steadily refuse all the glittering gifts and bribes which many politicians of both parties eagerly press upon you, if you will but accept them as your leaders, and lend them the power which your numbers can give. Enter into none of these corrupt and fatal compacts. . . .

See also another truth. There are few greater injuries that can be inflicted on you than taking out of your hands the great services that supply your wants. Why? Because the healing virtue that belongs to all these great services—education, religion, the winning of land and houses, the securing greater comfort and refinement and amusement in your lives—lies in the winning of these things for yourselves by your own exertions, through your own skill, your own courage, your friendly co-operation one with another, your integrity in your common dealings, your unconquerable self-reliance and confidence in your own powers of doing. This winning, these efforts, are the great lessons in life-long education; that lasts from childhood to the grave; and when learnt, they are learnt not for yourselves alone, but for your children, and your children's children. They are the steps and the only steps up to the higher levels. You can't be carried to those higher levels on the shoulders of others. The politician is like those who boasted to have the keys of earth and heaven in their pocket. Vainest of vain pretences! The keys both of heaven and earth lie in your own pocket; it is only you—you, the free individuals—who can unlock the great door. All these great wants and services are the means by which we acquire the great qualities which spell victory; they are the means by which we become raised and changed in ourselves, and by which, as we are changed, we change and remake all the circumstances of our lives. Each victory so gained prepares the way for the next victory, and makes that next victory the easier, for we not only have the sense of success in our hearts, but we have begun to acquire the qualities on which it depends. . . .

Refuse then to put your faith in mere machinery, in party organizations, in Acts of Parliament, in great unwieldy systems, which treat good and bad, the careful and the careless, the striving and the indifferent, on the same plan, and which on account of their vast and cumbrous size, their complexity, their official central management, pass entirely out of your control. Refuse to be spoon-fed, drugged and dosed, by the politicians. They are not leading you towards the promised land, but further and further away from it. If the world could be saved by the men of words and the machine-makers, it would have been saved long ago. Nothing is easier than to make machinery; you may have any quantity of it on order in a few months. Nothing is easier than to appoint any number of officials. Unluckily the true fight is of another and much sterner kind; and the victory comes of our own climbing of the hills, not by sitting in the plain, with folded hands, watching those others who profess to do our business for us. Do you think it likely or reasonable, do you think it fits in with and agrees with your daily experience of this fighting, working world of ours, that you could take your chair in the politician's shop, and order across his counter so much prosperity and progress and happiness, just as you might order cotton goods by the piece or wheat by the quarter? Be brave and clear-sighted, and face the stern but wholesome truth, that it is only you, you with your own hands, you with your unconquerable resolve, without any dependence on others, without any of these childish and mischievous party struggles, which are perhaps a little more exciting than cricket, or football, or even 'bridge' to some of us, but a good deal more profitless to the nation than digging holes in the earth and then filling them up again, without any use of force, without any oppression of each other, without any of these blind reckless attempts to humiliate and defeat those who hold different beliefs from ourselves, and who desire to follow different methods from those which we follow, without any division of the nation into two, three or more hostile camps, ever inspired with dread and hatred of each other—it is only you yourselves, fighting with the good, pure, honest weapons of persuasion and example, of sympathy and friendly co-operation—it is only you, calling out in yourselves the great qualities, and flinging away all the meaner things, the strifes, the hates, the jealousies, the mere love of fighting and conquering—it is only you, treading in the blessed path of peace and freedom, who can bring about the true regeneration of society, and with it the true happiness of your own lives.

And through it all avoid that favourite, that much loved snare of the politician, by which he ever seeks to rivet his hold upon you, refuse to attack and weaken in any manner the full rights of property. You, who are workers, could not inflict on your own selves a more fatal injury. Property is the great and good inducement that will call out your efforts and energies for the remaking of the present form of society. Deprive property of its full value and attractiveness, and we shall all become stuff only fit to make the helpless incapable crowd that the Socialist so deeply admires, and hopes so easily to control. But it is not only for the sake of the 'magic of property', its power to call out the qualities of industry and saving; it is above all because you cannot weaken the rights of property without diminishing, without injuring that first and greatest of all possessions—human liberty; it is for that supreme reason that we must resist every attempt of the politician to buy votes by generously giving away the property that does not belong to him. The control of his own property by the individual, and the liberty of the individual can never be separated from each other. They must stand, or fall, together. Property, when earned, is the product of faculties, and results from their free exercise; and, when inherited, represents the full right of a man, free from all imaginary and usurped control of others, to deal as he likes with his own. Destroy the rights of property, and you will also destroy both the material and the moral foundations of liberty. To all men and women, rich or poor, belong their own faculties, and as a consequence, equally belongs to them all that they can honestly gain in free and open competition, through the exercise of those faculties.

It is idle to talk of freedom, and, whilst the word is on one's lips, to attack property. He who attacks property, joins the camp of those who wish to keep some men in subjection to the will of others. You cannot break down any of the defences of liberty, you cannot weaken liberty at any one point, without weakening it at all points. Liberty means refusing to allow some men to use the State to compel other men to serve their interests or their opinions; and at whatever point we allow this servitude to exist, we weaken or destroy in men's minds the sacredness of the principle, which must be, as regards all actions, all relations, our universal bond. But it is not only for the sake of liberty—though that is far the greater and higher reason— it is also for the sake of your own material progress—that you, the workers, must resolutely reject all interference with, all mutilations of the rights of property....

. . .Resist, therefore, all reckless, unthinking appeals made to you to deprive the great prize of any part of its attractions. If you surround property with State restrictions, interfere with free trade and any part of the open market, interfere with free contract, make compulsory arrangements for tenant and landowner, allow the present burdens of rate and tax to discourage ownership and penalize improvements, you will weaken the motives for acquiring property, and blunt the edge of the most powerful material instrument that exists for your own advancement. Only remember—as we have said—that great as is your material interest in safeguarding the rights of individual property, yet higher and greater are and ever will be the moral reasons that forbid our sanctioning any attack upon it, or our suffering State burdens and restrictions and impediments to grow round it. True liberty— as we said—cannot exist apart from the full rights of property; for property is—so to speak—only the crystallized form of free faculties. . . .

. . .Establish freedom and open competition in everything, and all forms of trade and enterprise, all relations of men to each other, tend to become healthy and vigorous, pure and clean. The better and more efficient forms—as they do throughout nature's world—slowly displacing the inefficient forms. It must be so; for in the fair open fight the good always tend to win over the bad, if only you restrain all interferences of force. It is so with freedom everywhere and in all things. Freedom begets the conflict; the conflict begets the good and helpful qualities; and the good and helpful qualities win their own victory. They must do so; for they are in themselves stronger, more energetic, more efficient, than the forces—the trickeries, the corruptions, the timidities, the self-ishness—to which they are opposed. The same truth rules our good and bad habits. Only keep the field open and allow the fair fight, and the bad at last must yield to the good. Sooner or later the time comes when the clearer sighted, the more rightly judging few denounce some evil habit that exists; gradually their influ-ence and example act on others in ever-widening circles, until many men grow ashamed of what they have so long done, and the habit is abandoned. Such is the universal law of progress, which prevails in everything, so long as we allow the free open fight between all good and evil. But in order that the good may prevail there must be life and vigour in the people, and this can only be where freedom exists. . . .

And now place before yourselves the picture of the nation that not simply out of self-interest but for rights' sake and conscience sake took to its heart the great cause of true liberty, and was de-termined that all men and women should be left free to guide themselves and take charge of their own lives; that was deter-mined to oppress and persecute and restrain the actions of no single person in order to serve any interest or any opinion or any class advantage; that flung out of its hands the bad instrument of force—using force only for its one clear, simple and rightful purpose of restraining all acts of force and fraud, committed by one citizen against another, of safeguarding the lives, the actions, the property of all, and thus making a fair open field for all honest effort; think, under the influences of liberty and her twin-sister peace—for they are inseparably bound together—neither existing without the other—how our character as a people would grow nobler and at the same time softer and more generous— think how the old useless enmities and jealousies and strivings would die out; how the unscrupulous politician would become a reformed character, hardly recognizing his old self in his new and better self; how men of all classes would learn to co-operate together for every kind of good and useful purpose; how, as the results of this free co-operation, innumerable ties of friendship and kindliness would spring up amongst us all of every class and condition, when we no longer sought to humble and crush each other, but invited all who were willing to work freely with us; how much truer and more real would be the campaign against the be-setting vices and weakness of our nature, when we sought to change that nature, not simply to tie men's hands and restrain external action, no longer setting up and establishing in all parts of life that poor weak motive –the fear of punishment—those clumsy useless penalties, evaded and laughed at by the cunning, that have never yet turned sinner into saint; how we should re-discover in ourselves the good vigorous stuff that lies hidden there, the power to plan, to dare and to do; how we should see in clearer light our duty towards other nations, and fulfil more faithfully our great world-trust; how we should cease to be a peo-ple divided into three or four quarrelsome unscrupulous factions—ready to sacrifice all the great things to their intense de-sire for power—and grow into a people really one in heart and mind, because we frankly recognized the right to differ, the right of each one to choose his own path because we respected and cherished the will, the intelligence, the free choice of others, as much as we respect and cherish these things in ourselves, and were resolved never to trample, for the sake of any plea, for any motive, on the higher parts of human nature, resolved that—come storm or sunshine—we would not falter in our allegiance to liberty and her sister peace, that we would do all, dare all, and suffer all, if need be, for their sake, then at last the regeneration of society would begin, the real promised land, not the imaginary land of vain and mocking desires, would be in sight. . . .

PART FIVE

RELIGIOUS INDIVIDUALISM

21. FROM *THE ESSENTIAL RIGHTS AND LIBERTIES OF PROTESTANTS*

ELISHA WILLIAMS

The Essential Rights and Liberties of Protestants. A Seasonable Plea for the Liberty of Conscience, and the Right of Private Judgment, in Matters of Religion. (Boston: S. Kneeland and T. Green, 1744)

Elisha Williams (1665–1755), a Yale graduate, served in the Connecticut General Assembly, as a judge on the Connecticut Supreme Court, and as a delegate to the Albany Congress in 1754. In this passage from The Essential Rights and Liberties of Protestants, *we find one of the best 18th-century discussions of the inalienable right of conscience, a key element of religious individualism.*

Every man has an equal right to follow the dictates of his own conscience in the affairs of religion. Every one is under an indispensable obligation to search the scripture for himself (which contains the whole of it) and to make the best use of it he can for his own information in the will of GOD, the nature and duties of Christianity. And as every Christian is so bound; so he has an unalienable right to judge of the sense and meaning of it, and to follow his judgment wherever it leads him; even an equal right with any rulers be they civil or ecclesiastical. This I say, I take to be an original right of the humane nature, and so far from being given up by the individuals of a community that it cannot be given up by them if they should be so weak as to offer it. Man by his constitution as he is a reasonable being capable of the knowledge of his Maker; is a moral & accountable being: and therefore as every one is accountable for himself, he must reason, judge and determine for himself. That faith and practice which depends on the judgment and choice of any other person, and not on the person's own understanding judgment and choice, may pass for religion in the synagogue of Satan, whose tenet is that ignorance is the mother of devotion; but with no understanding Protestant will it pass for any religion at all. No action is a religious action without understanding and choice in the agent. Whence it follows, the rights of conscience are sacred and equal in all, and strictly speaking unalienable. This *right of judging every one for himself in matters of religion* results from the nature of man, and is so inseperably connected therewith, that a man can no more part with it than he can with his power of thinking: and it is equally reasonable for him to attempt to strip himself of the power of reasoning, as to attempt the vesting of another with this right. And whoever invades this right of another, be he pope or Cæsar, may with equal reason assume the other's power of thinking, and so level him with the brutal creation. A man may alienate some branches of his property and give up his right in them to others; but he cannot transfer the rights of conscience, unless he could destroy his rational and moral powers, or substitute some other to be judged for him at the tribunal of GOD.

22. FROM "FREE THOUGHT—ITS CONDITIONS, AGREEMENTS, AND SECULAR RESULTS"

GEORGE JACOB HOLYOAKE

The Reasoner, April 1872

George Jacob Holyoake (1817–1906) was an English Chartist, Owenite, and freethinker. He promoted voluntary socialism, educational opportunities for all social classes, and "secularism," a term he coined. He served six months in prison on charges of blasphemy. Holyoake crusaded for the right of every individual to freedom of thought, inquiry, and speech. The following excerpt from "Free Thought—Its Conditions, Agreements, and Secular Results" was published in The Reasoner, *a weekly journal of freethought that Holyoake founded in 1846 and edited for 15 years.*

Free Thought signifies the unrestricted application of the powers of the intellect to any subject. It means the absence of any threat, or penalty, or impediment to the exercise of thought. The application of thought to any subject may be unsatisfactory—no result may be arrived at—a disagreeable discovery may be made—the end of the investigation may be worthless, or painful, or offensive, and it may be desirable to beat a retreat from it as soon as it is reached: but the right to reach it and gain that experience must be undisputed before Free Thought can be said to exist. To be a Free-Thinker in any proper sense of the term there must be no fetter on the mind—no fear in the use of thought, and no dread of any result. There must be no intention, or desire, or anxiety, to make a result arrived at agree with the Bible, for instance, or to agree with or corroborate any foregone conclusion. There must be no dread of God's displeasure at the honest result—there must be no effective social penalty, or censure, or disapprobation at the exercise of thought, or it cannot be free. Free Thought is an instrument, as it were, of investigation. It will not insure to all the same ultimate results, but it affords them the best chance of attaining the truth. All men have not equal strength of mind in using Free Thought—all do not employ it upon the same facts, or materials, or premises of argument. Free Thought may land some in heresy, some in mere Theism, some in Atheism. Yet there are certain primary and secular things into which all are led who employ intelligently the principle of Free Thought. Free Thought is a primary principle, from which several things flow, which all who intelligently stand on the side of Free Thought perceive, accept, and act upon. On the very threshold of the term Free Thought we find three ideas included in it, namely—

The Necessity of Free Thought.
The Rightfulness of it.
The Adequacy of it.

1. *Its Necessity.*—All men love freedom naturally. It is an instinct of their nature. It is the condition of growth and development. There can be no progress without it. All art, all science, all improvement is owing to the use of it. Every new religion has been created by it. Christ and his Apostles employed it to a great extent. Men would have dwelt in ignorance and superstition without it. Freedom of thought is a necessity of progressive life. Every man would be at the mercy of falsehood, of knavery, of speech, of fanaticism, of wanton speculation and fatal error—unless he fell back on his own judgment and defended himself. Free Thought is

self-defence, as well as a necessity. If we are responsible to society or to God, Free Thought is a moral obligation; a duty as well as a right.

2. *Its Rightfulness.*—That which is a necessity of intellectual existence and a moral obligation can be no crime. If God has made us, He has put His stamp of approval on Free Thought, for he has made it the deepest instinct of intelligence and the means of all excellence. Yet it would be impossible if men believed it to be a guilty thing, for no sane men would then venture upon it. If ignorance were felt to be innocence, no well-disposed person would attempt to get knowledge. But experience tells us that ignorance is a misfortune or an offence; therefore Free Thought, which dispels ignorance and is the prime creator of knowledge, must be a virtue.

3. *Its Adequacy.*—Every Free Thinker commences by assuming the comparative sufficiency of reason as an instrument of investigation. Free Thought is simply the free employment of reason in the conduct of life. Every Free Thinker necessarily believes in the practical adequacy of this instrument. Free Thought is the following of reason, which it sets up as the test of the Bible, of Christianity, of authority. Free Thought does not begin in the rebellion but in the action or the understanding; with a view to self-protection and to truth. Reason, the faculty of following the path of facts, does not despise intuition, or instinct, or the voice of nature, or authority—it uses but revises them. It does not pretend to be infallible, or all sufficient in an absolute sense, but Reason is the supreme arbiter, and the most reliable arbiter we have for the conduct of life. It is not perfect, but yet supreme. It is the high court of the understanding, beyond which there is no appeal. Compared with all other

means of judgment, all Free Thinkers agree in giving it the first place of efficiency, sufficiency, and adequacy.

If Free Thought be therefore a needful, rightful, and adequate instrument of progress, it implies whatever is necessary for its existence and operation; it implies further—

The Free Publication of well-intentioned Thought.
The Fair Criticism of it.
The Equal Action of Conviction.

4. *Free Publicity.*—The free publication of presumedly useful opinion by tongue and pen, is essential to Free Thought. Logicians prove that reasoning itself is impossible without the use of words as the instrument of it. Without publicity of ideas society could never be benefited by the labours of successful thinkers. No man can preserve his own sanity who is denied conversation with his fellows. Without the comparison of ideas with those of other men, no man can either be sure of the truth or escape lunacy. All great thinkers who are isolated, or who are much before their age, and have no equals with whom they can test the truth of their views, are partially insane, or are believed to be so, or are treated as such. The right of publication of well-considered opinion is one of the high conditions of intellectual progress and sanity to all men.

The greatest absurdity of speech arises from persons not being taught that mere talk is wind and worthlessness. Unless there is purpose and relevance in speech, it is of no consequence in advocacy. Truth itself requires discrimination in its use. People constantly overlook that what is true is not always useful. A man may know a thousand things that are true, but still trivial, or mischievous, or defamatory.

The most liberal laws distinguish between well-intentioned and malicious truth. Chaffers, who assailed Lady Twiss, was assumed to have some truth to tell, but he was deemed not less infamous on that account. We contend for the right of publicity of that truth which is relevant and presumptively useful to society.

5. *Fair Criticism.*—Without Fair Criticism, thought could never be tested or improved. Thought is often foolish, often mischievous, and sometimes wicked; but he alone who submits it to free criticism gives guarantees to society that he means well, though he may be in error, since Criticism must bring down upon him exposure and punishment if he be in fault or foolish. He who perverts Free-thinking into loose thinking—he who degrades free speech to a scream of passion, or makes it an echo of folly, is a traitor to both, and Criticism is the Court where the treason is tried and punished. Criticism is the corrector of erroneous thought or abuse of freedom. The liberty of Criticism is a limitation of free speech, imposing upon it reflection and care; and Criticism itself has conditions, namely, those of seeking less to assail error than to discover and establish truth—less to intensify the differences which divide men than to discover the agreements which may further unite them. Fair Criticism respects the aims of the thinker criticized.

6. *Equal Action of Conviction.*—Without the reasonable action of opinion, thought is practically fruitless. We must be able to embody ideas in institutions. There must be fair play for thought as well as free play. The Free-Thinker must have equal civil rights, and be free to live a life in accordance with his convictions, provided he respects the equal rights of others in doing so. There must be an end of civil disqualifi-

cations for honest opinion. The new law of Secular Affirmations provides that the heretic shall have equal right of protection in law with the Christian. There can be no free action of opinion without equal civil rights.

Free Thought without limits is license; and publication, debate and action may prove offensive and barren of moral results. The savage is the type of brute liberty, which includes plunder and murder amongst his pastimes. This sentiment is that oft-quoted one from the conquest of Granada, which Dryden puts into the mouth of Almanyor:—

> "I am as free as Nature first made man,
> Ere the base laws of servitude began,
> When wild in woods the noble savage ran."

When a limit is first put to this by civilization, many men gradually lose the instinct of freedom. Obedience to authority becomes implicit. Society degenerates into slavery of person and mind—and men arise who preach that freedom of thought itself is a crime, and all conduct which does not conform to the second-rate notions of a man's commonplace neighbours, is treated as a social offence. Temperate individuality becomes nearly impossible. Two classes of men, then, in due course, disturb or disgrace the state—one who assert freedom in the form of outrage, another who suffer obedience to subside into submission. These are they, who, as politicians, invent systems of officious centralisation, and treat Government as so much machinery for rendering liberty impossible. The Free-Thinker, guided by his own leading principle, seeks that limit to free action which shall preserve individuality in the midst of society, and reconcile order and independence.

23. FROM "INDIVIDUALITY"

ROBERT G. INGERSOLL

The Gods and Other Lectures (Washington, DC: C. P. Farrell, 1879)

Robert Green Ingersoll (1833–99), an icon of American freethought, was an attorney, abolitionist, Republican politician, and orator who served in the Illinois Volunteer Calvary during the Civil War. Ingersoll defended the absolute separation of church and state, and freedom in matters of conscience. He promoted the acceptance of agnosticism and became known as "The Great Infidel." Ingersoll was a renowned orator, and most of his works were originally delivered as speeches. In the following passage, Ingersoll argues for the importance of individuality to civilization.

It is a blessed thing that in every age some one has had individuality enough and courage enough to stand by his own convictions—some one who had the grandeur to say his say. I believe it was Magellan who said, "The Church says the earth is flat; but I have seen its shadow on the moon, and I have more confidence even in a shadow than in the Church." On the prow of his ship were disobedience, defiance, scorn, and success. . . .

. . .Whoever believes at the command of power, tramples his own individuality beneath his feet and voluntarily robs himself of all that renders man superior to the brute. . . .

All that is good in our civilization is the result of commerce, climate, soil, geographical position, industry, invention, discovery, art, and science. The Church has been the enemy of progress, for the reason that it has endeavored to prevent man thinking for himself. To prevent thought is to prevent all advancement except in the direction of faith.

Who can imagine the infinite impudence of a Church assuming to think for the human race? Who can imagine the infinite impudence of a Church that pretends to be the mouthpiece of God, and in his name threatens to inflict eternal punishment upon those who honestly reject its claims and scorn its pretensions? By what right does a man, or an organization of men, or a god, claim to hold a brain in bondage? When a fact can be demonstrated, force is unnecessary; when it cannot be demonstrated, an appeal to force is infamous. In the presence of the unknown all have an equal right to think.

Over the vast plain, called life, we are all travelers, and not one traveler is perfectly certain that he is going in the right direction. True it is that no other plain is so well supplied with guide-boards. At every turn and crossing you will find them, and upon each one is written the exact direction and distance. One great trouble is, however, that these boards are all different, and the result is that most travelers are confused in proportion to the number they read. Thousands of people are around each of these signs, and each one is doing his best to convince the traveler that his particular board is the only one upon which the least reliance can be placed, and that if his road is taken the reward for so doing will be infinite and eternal, while all the other roads are said to lead to hell, and all the makers of the other guide-boards are declared to be heretics, hypocrites and liars. "Well," says a traveler, "you may be right in what you say, but allow me at least to read some of the other directions and examine a little into their claims. I wish to rely a little upon my own judgment in a matter of so great importance." "No, sir," shouts the zealot, "that is the very thing you are not allowed to do. You must go my way without investigation, or you are as good as damned already." "Well," says the traveler, "if that is so, I believe I had better go your way." And so most of them go along, taking the word of those who know as little as themselves. Now and then comes one who, in spite of all threats, calmly examines the claims of all, and as calmly rejects them all. These travelers take roads of their own, and are denounced by all the others, as infidels and atheists. . . .

In my judgment, every human being should take a road of his own. Every mind should be true to itself—should think, investigate and conclude for itself. This is a duty alike incumbent upon pauper and prince. Every soul should repel dictation and tyranny, no matter from what source they come—from earth or heaven, from men or gods. Besides, every traveler upon this vast plain should give to every other traveler his best idea as to the road that should be taken. Each is entitled to the honest opinion of all. And there is but one way to get an honest opinion upon any subject whatever. The person giving the opinion must be free from fear. The merchant must not fear to lose his custom, the doctor his practice, nor the preacher his pulpit. There can be no advance without liberty. Suppression of honest inquiry is retrogression, and must end in intellectual night. The tendency of orthodox religion to-day is toward mental slavery and barbarism. Not one of the orthodox ministers dare preach what he thinks if he knows a majority of his congregation think otherwise. He knows that every member of his church stands guard over his brain with a creed, like a club, in his hand. He knows that he is not expected to search after the truth, but that he is employed to defend the creed. Every pulpit is a pillory, in which stands a hired culprit, defending the justice of his own imprisonment.

Is it desirable that all should be exactly alike in their religious convictions? Is any such thing possible? Do we not know that there are no two persons alike in the whole world? No two trees, no two leaves, no two anythings that are alike? Infinite diversity is the law. Religion tries to force all minds into one mould. Knowing that all cannot believe, the Church endeavors to make all say they believe. She longs for the unity of hypocrisy, and detests the splendid diversity of individuality and freedom.

Nearly all people stand in great horror of annihilation, and yet to give up your individuality is to annihilate yourself. Mental slavery is mental death, and every man who has given up his intellectual freedom is the living coffin of his dead soul. . . .

We should all remember that to be like other people is to be unlike ourselves, and that nothing can be more detestable in character than servile imitation. The great trouble with imitation is, that we are apt to ape those who are in reality far below us. After all, the poorest bargain that a human being can make, is to give his individuality for what is called respectability.

There is no saying more degrading than this: "It is better to be the tail of a lion than the head of a dog." It is a responsibility to think and act for yourself. Most people hate responsibility; therefore they join something and become the tail of some lion. They say, "My party can act for me—my church can do my thinking. It is enough for me to pay taxes and obey the lion to which I belong, without troubling myself about the right, the wrong, or the why or the wherefore of anything whatever." These people are respectable. They hate reformers, and dislike exceedingly to have their minds disturbed. They regard convictions as very disagreeable things to have. They love forms, and enjoy, beyond everything else, telling what a splendid tail their lion has, and what a troublesome dog their neighbor is. Besides this natural inclination to avoid personal responsibility, is and always has been, the fact, that every religionist has warned men against the presumption and wickedness of thinking for themselves. The reason has been denounced by all Christendom as the only unsafe guide. The Church has left nothing undone to prevent man following the logic of his brain. The plainest facts have been covered with the mantle of mystery. The grossest absurdities have been declared to be self-evident facts. The order of nature has been, as it were, reversed, that the hypocritical few might govern the honest many. The man who stood by the conclusion of his reason was denounced as a scorner and hater of God and his holy Church. From the organization of the first Church until this moment, to think your own thoughts has been inconsistent with membership. Every member has borne the marks of collar, and chain, and whip. No man ever seriously attempted to reform a Church without being cast out and hunted down by the hounds of hypocrisy. The highest crime against a creed is to change it. Reformation is treason. . . .

There can be nothing more utterly subversive of all that is really valuable than the suppression of honest thought. No man, worthy of the form he bears, will at the command of Church or State solemnly repeat a creed his reason scorns.

It is the duty of each and every one to maintain his individuality. "This above all, to thine own-self be true, and it must follow as the night the day, thou canst not then be false to any man." It is a magnificent thing to be the sole proprietor of yourself. It is a terrible thing to wake up at night and say, "There is nobody in this bed." It is humiliating to know that your ideas are all borrowed; that you are indebted to your memory for your principles; that your religion is simply one of your habits, and that you would have convictions if they were only contagious. It is

mortifying to feel that you belong to a mental mob and cry "cru-
cify him," because the others do; that you reap what the great and
brave have sown, and that you can benefit the world only by
leaving it.

Surely every human being ought to attain to the dignity of the
unit. Surely it is worth something to be *one,* and to feel that the
census of the universe would be incomplete without counting
you. Surely there is grandeur in knowing that in the realm of
thought, at least, you are without a chain; that you have the right
to explore all heights and all depths; that there are no walls nor
fences, nor prohibited places, nor sacred corners in all the vast
expanse of thought; that your intellect owes no allegiance to any
being, human or divine; that you hold all in fee and upon no condition and by no tenure whatever; that in the world of mind you
are relieved from all personal dictation, and from the ignorant
tyranny of majorities. Surely it is worth something to feel that
there are no priests, no popes, no parties, no governments, no
kings, no gods, to whom your intellect can be compelled to pay a
reluctant homage. Surely it is a joy to know that all the cruel in-
genuity of bigotry can devise no prison, no dungeon, no cell in
which for one instant to confine a thought; that ideas cannot be
dislocated by racks, nor crushed in iron boots, nor burned with
fire. Surely it is sublime to think that the brain is a castle, and
within its curious bastions and winding halls the soul, in spite of
all worlds and all beings, is the supreme sovereign of itself.

PART SIX

ECONOMIC INDIVIDUALISM

HENRY WILSON

A Catechism of Individualism (London: The Liberty Review Publishing Company, 1902)

Henry Wilson, a lieutenant colonel in the British army, was a frequent contributor to The Liberty Review *(published by the Liberty and Property Defence League) until he was killed in a bicycle accident on January 8, 1907. He was secretary of the Individualist Club, treasurer of the Personal Rights Association, and a contributor to Auberon Herbert's periodical,* Free Life. *In the booklet reprinted here in its entirety, Wilson responds to* A New Catechism of Socialism, *which was written by the English journalist and philosopher Belfort Bax in collaboration with his friend Henry Quelch.*

What do you understand by Individualism?
It is the opposite of Socialism.

Why do you give this negative definition?
Because Individualism is the natural system, and would never have got a distinctive name, or have had to search for its principles, and the reasons on which they are founded, but for the rise of the artificial system of Socialism.

Am I to understand, then, that Individualism is the earlier of the two systems?
No. Modern Socialism is an attempt to give a scientific justification for a barbarous stage through which men passed in their upward struggle to their present happier state.

Why do you call Socialism artificial?

Because man always, if left free, passes from Socialism to Individualism, at least in the more advanced races. His happiness and prosperity are in proportion to the completeness of the change. Socialism is an attempt to set back the clock, and forcibly to re-introduce barbarism.

What, then, are these two opposite systems?

They are systems for the arrangement of society wholly in the field of *economics*.

Why do you lay stress on the word "economics"?

Because there is a very common error among inaccurate thinkers, seen even in so eminent a writer as Ruskin, that these systems have something to do with ethics. Mr. Bax, in his "Catechism of Socialism," devotes a chapter to the Ethics of Socialism. But Socialism has no ethics. A Socialist may have—he may be an Intuitionist or a Utilitarian, just as he might be an Allopathist or a Homœopathist, but he might as well talk of the ethics of astronomy or chemistry as of the ethics of socialism.

What, then, is the distinction between ethics on the one hand and economics, chemistry, physics, etc., on the other?

Ethics gives orders, the other sciences state facts.

How has the confusion arisen in the case of ethics and economics?

Probably in this way. They both deal with human motives and actions.

What is the difference in their treatment?

Ethics tells me what *ought* to be *my* motives and *my* actions. Economics tells me what *are other* men's motives, and what *will be* their actions.

Can you give an example of this confusion from a well-known writer?

Ruskin quotes a saying of Adam Smith, that the real check on a tradesman is his customer. He characterises this as the most bestial utterance he ever heard. It is plain, then, that when Adam Smith made the economic statement, that a tradesman *was* induced to sell good wares for fear of losing customers, Ruskin took him to make the ethical statement, that his sole reason for being honest *ought* to be the fear of losing customers. And when Ruskin goes on to say that in his ideal state every baker should belong to a guild, which should sternly punish him if he sold short weight, he furnishes a delightful instance of inconsistency.

Then ethics cannot move till these other sciences have had their say?

Exactly. When chemistry has told me that nitric acid thrown in a person's face will cause great agony; when physics has told me that throwing a person out of a window will tend to cause broken bones or death; when economics has told me that promising to keep a person in old age will make him idle and improvident, then, and not till then, can ethics step in and forbid me to commit those actions.

Can you give a definition of Socialism?

This is the definition given by Mr. Belfort Bax in his "Catechism of Socialism": "The system of society the material basis of which is social production for social use."

Have you any objection to make to this definition?
The coat I wear and the beefsteak I eat are used by me individually, not socially.

Supposing the definition were altered to "Social production for individual use," would you still object?
Yes. Men have produced socially for individual use ever since civilization began. In fact, that is civilization. If twenty men agree to form a society, community, or tribe, Brown agrees to make all the shoes for the community, Jones all the coats, and so on. That, if a voluntary arrangement, is individualistic.

Where, then, does the difference between Socialism and Individualism come in?
Chiefly in the distribution. Though I believe Socialism would control the number of shoes Brown produces, instead of leaving it to Brown to estimate the demand.

Then are there two questions involved?
There are—production and distribution. First, how many shoes and coats Brown and Jones shall make; and, secondly, how many shoes Brown the shoemaker shall give Jones the tailor for a coat.

How is this settled under the system of Individualism?
By leaving Brown and Jones to gauge the demand for their respective goods, under the stimulus of self-interest, their living depending on a right estimate; and by assuming that every man is the best judge of what he wants and its value to him, and leaving the matter to be settled by bargaining.

What are the advantages of this system?

The question is settled automatically and without expense. Both parties gain, and both are satisfied.

Are there any drawbacks?

No human institution is perfect. Brown or Jones may overestimate or underestimate the demand, so that there will be some loss to one of the parties.

How is it settled under the system of Socialism?

It could only be settled by appointing some central authority to tell Brown, first, how many shoes he is to make, and, secondly, how many he is to give Jones for a coat.

What are the drawbacks to this plan?

It shifts the duty of estimating the needs of the community from a responsible person, who would suffer if he judged wrongly, to an irresponsible person, who would not suffer. Also this person would have to be paid, which burden would fall on all the other members. Also, as he could not possibly gauge the value of anything, he would certainly not satisfy one of the exchangers, and probably would satisfy neither. Moreover, as production would be limited to supposed needs, the power of choice would be much curtailed for the consumer.

Would the system have any advantages?

It is claimed for it that it would save the expenses of advertising, commercial travellers, and such like. Also that things would be produced which are not now, because they afford no profit—that is, are so little desired that people will not give enough for them to afford a profit.

You used the word "value." What meaning do you attach to that word?

The power of satisfying man's desires.

Is this a quality inherent in things and constant?

Certainly not. It varies with each individual man, with the same man from year to year and from hour to hour. A man of sixty does not value a top as he did when he was six, nor does a man who has just dined value a loaf of bread as much as one does who has fasted twelve hours.

How is value measured?

By the pain or annoyance that would be caused by the absence of the last increment of the thing in question.

Give an example.

A man at dinner values a morsel of food by the annoyance he would feel if he had not got it, not by his wish for the next morsel, for if he has had enough he attaches no value to the next morsel.

What is this called?

The marginal value of a thing—that is a man's estimate of its marginal utility.

But is not this difficult to express definitely?

It is. In practice we estimate the value of a thing by the amount of something else which a man has and will give up rather than forego the thing in question.

Would not this amount vary with the nature of the something else he gives up?

It would. Men usually fix on some one thing in which to estimate the value of all others. This one thing is called a medium of exchange, and value as expressed in it is called price.

Do not some writers, like Ruskin, say that value is inherent in a thing?

They do. Ruskin says that a picture by Botticelli has inherent value, while a cask of whisky has not only no value, but has, so to speak, a minus value.

What is your comment on this?

On analyzing this statement I find that value is still a matter of opinion, only it is Ruskin's opinion of what satisfies *his* desires, instead of the opinion of those concerned of what satisfies *their* desires.

Then it is not an economic utterance?

No. It confuses economics, which investigates what men *do* like, with Ruskin's sociology which lays down what he thinks they *ought* to like.

Had Ruskin an amusing proof of this in his own experience?

He had. He wrote a number of works, eloquently laying down what he thought right conduct, which works he thought valuable. But twice the editor of a magazine had to refuse his articles, for fear of their ruining the magazine.

Then what would have been Ruskin's position under the system of State regulation which he advocated?

He would have been utterly refused a hearing.

Is, then, the value of anything never constant?

If the demand for anything is very great, and it is either very durable or can be produced in great quantities, its value tends to be constant.

Can you give examples?

Gold is an instance of the first, and bread of the second. Bread is perishable; but the ratio between the number of loaves on sale and the number of men who want to buy remains without change over considerable periods.

Then there seems to be a connection between the number and frequency of exchanges of a thing and the steadiness of its value?

A direct connection as Mr. Cree has shown. A loaf of bread, in which thousands of exchanges take place every day, remains very constant in value. A picture by an old master changes hands once in twenty years, and its price cannot be guessed by many thousand pounds.

To what do Socialists attribute value?

To the amount of labour a thing has cost.

Does this agree with facts?

A thing that is valuable has generally cost labour, which is the result of value, not the cause of it.

How do you know that?

A thing men do not wish for has no value, however much labour it has cost. A thing men desire intensely has much value, however little labour it has cost.

Give an example.
Two men shall spend the same number of years learning to paint, and then spend the same number of hours in painting a picture. One picture is worth £5, the other £5,000.

Do not people speak of different kinds of value?
Economists have sometimes spoken of value in use as different from value in exchange, speaking of iron as being useful, and gold as being useless.

Is this an error?
It springs from two errors. One is confusing, like Ruskin, what you think people ought to value with what they do value. Men all the world over are prone to value things which minister to show (like gold) more than things that minister to bodily needs (like iron). Again, much confusion arises from speaking of the value of gold or iron. Gold, iron, and bread have no value in the abstract. A particular piece of one of them may have value, according to the circumstances. In the Sahara a loaf of bread might be worth many times its weight in gold, and Robinson Crusoe might have been glad to give a large lump of gold for an iron knife.

How do you sum up the difference between the two systems of Individualism and Socialism?
Individualism throws on each man the responsibility of choosing a calling, fixing on the number of hours he shall work, the price of his goods, and the provision he shall make for the future of himself and his family. Socialism has all these fixed by Government.

Is a socialistic State possible?

In a community like a monastery, where food and clothing are coarse and uniform—above all, where all are unmarried, Socialism may be successfully practised.

The difference, then, between the two systems seems to turn on the amount of Government interference with individuals?

It does. Individualism limits the action of Government to repressing violence and fraud, and doing those things which, being everybody's business, are nobody's business.

How, then, are all social wants provided for under this system?

By making the doer of a service earn his living by what the receiver gives him freely. It is each man's interest to find out who wants a service, and to supply it well.

This system, then, throws the maximum of responsibility on individuals?

It does.

It appears, then, to be the same thing as freedom?

It is.

Socialism, then, must be the same thing as slavery?

Just so. The essence of slavery is absence of responsibility.

But do Socialists acknowledge this?

Clear-headed ones, like Ruskin, do. A Socialist writer, Mr. J. A. Hobson, remarks that Ruskin often turns aside to praise slavery.

Would not Government acting like a providence have a tendency to make men thoughtless, and leave everything to it?
It would, as we had a striking example in Paris not long ago. A fire broke out in a crowded bazaar, and many persons were burnt to death. One of the managers publicly repudiated all responsibility, and said that it was the fault of Government for not compelling them to provide means of rapid and orderly exit.

Is the system called Socialism well named?
Quite the contrary. It is a system of anti-social conduct; and Individualism contributes just as much to the welfare of society as to that of the individual.

But ought not the majority to rule the minority?
Only with regard to conduct hurtful to the majority. If two men are in a boat, it cannot sail both east and west at once. It must do one or the other. Now, if one of the two wants to put out to sea in a storm, the other, whose life would be endangered, has a right to resist. But that does not give him a right to interfere with the first man's religion, or dress, or the way he spends his time, so long as it is not spent in hindering the second. Then, if ninety-nine others, like minded with the second, enter the boat, that gives them no right to interfere with the first man that the second did not possess when alone. That is the A, B, C of liberty.

But do not Socialists complain that society now is unorganised?
They do, but it is a pure delusion. "Organised" means arranged like an organism. The human body is an organism. In it digestion, assimilation, nutrition, and expulsion of waste—processes which correspond to the feeding, clothing, travelling, and other activities of society—go on normally not only without the interference of

the brain, which is the government, but without its knowledge. If, then, the five millions in London get without fail daily their milk, bread, papers, and everything they want without the interference of government, society in London is organized. Also in a free society government is carried on by certain units elected by the others for a definite and limited purpose. The cells of the brain are not elected by the cells of the bones and muscles. In a society the life of the units is higher and more varied than that of the whole; in an organism it is just the reverse.

But Socialists say that production is now carried on in the interest and for the profit of the class that owns the means of production.

Anyone can see the falsity of that statement. There are producers in my village who own neither land, house, nor factory, nor anything but such tools as they have bought with their savings as wage earners. The mightiest businesses have all had a similar origin.

Then there is no such class as the Socialists speak of, bound together by a common interest against the rest of society?

Certainly not. Every member of the supposed class produces one thing, but consumes a thousand. Even if his interest in the one thing were opposed to that of the rest of society, his interest in the other thousand is at one with that of the rest of society.

What is the Socialist definition of capital?

This is a summary of Mr. Bax's definition—a good example of the way in which Socialists mix morals with economics: A "considerable concentration of the means of production in the hands of one or a few persons, who employ others to produce and keep the product, paying only a small proportion to the producers."

What strikes you in this definition?
The appeals to prejudice. Capital is not recognized as such unless it is large, and in the hands of a few, who treat their workmen unjustly.

What is capital really?
Produce saved, whether little or much, and used to produce more wealth, whether by the owner or by others.

What is wealth?
Anything that has value.

You said value was the power of satisfying human desire.
I did. That implies that a valuable thing is limited in quantity, for no one would desire a particular mouthful of air if he could get another as good for nothing.

Can air ever have value?
Yes, in the Black Hole of Calcutta, as a draught of water is valuable in the desert or in a large town.

Socialists attribute value to the average labour which a thing has cost, do they not?
Yes, following an unfortunate mistake of Adam Smith and Ricardo. They deify labour and think, like Charles Lamb's friend, that they could write as good plays as Shakespeare's if they had a mind.

What example does Mr. Bax give?
He supposes a man wishing to exchange a pair of boots for a quarter of wheat, and assumes that his anxiety is to get the same amount of labour in return that the boots cost him.

Why is this not so?

The wheat would cost the bootmaker much more labour than the boots have, and he has no means of knowing how much it cost the farmer. A great many things derive their excellence from inborn qualities, without labour, which no labour can give, like a singer's voice.

So it is not even true that, as Mr. Bax says, the labour spent on each side, take all bargains together, balances?

No; and even if it were, the labour would be the result of the value, not the cause of it. But the voice and ear of a singer, the touch of a player, the eye of a painter, the imagination of a poet, even the taste of a tailor or milliner, are not, and cannot be, the result of labour.

Does not Mr. Bax complain that things are made now for exchange, not for use?

He does; but that is only the result of the division of labour, whereby men get many more satisfactions, by each making one thing and exchanging.

How would Socialists manage it?

They would have everything sent into a Government warehouse, and served out in return for tickets or orders. That would only shift the estimate of value from the parties concerned to a Government official. How much bread would he value Mr. Bax's catechism at?

How does Mr. Bax explain profit?

In the queerest way. He says profit cannot be made on the market, for as the sum of satisfactions or profits on each side must, in the long run, balance, there can be no profit. Now, as profit is what every producer for exchange lives on, everyone must be dead.

That sounds singular reasoning.
It is quite normal Socialist reasoning. A bootmaker, having provided for his own wear, exchanges the other boots he makes for wheat, mutton, coats, and everything necessary to support life, and the farmer does the same with his spare wheat, and this goes on for seventy years. Yet, according to Mr. Bax, they are dead all the time.

How has the error arisen?
Mr. Bax says that it is impossible to make a profit by exchange, for to do that you must sell above the cost of production, and that is impossible if the accounts balance. He does not see that we measure our profits, not in sovereigns, but in the satisfaction of our desires. If I get a pound of tea from a Chinaman in return for a yard of cotton, the tea which I had not gives me more pleasure than the cotton of which I had enough already. So I sell at a profit. In the same way the Chinaman values the cotton more than the tea, of which he had enough and to spare. So he sells at a profit. The accounts balance, and yet we are alive!

How do Socialists say profit is made?
By a curious and fantastic thing called surplus value. This is very important, for, as Mr. Bax says, in this is "the kernel of the whole capitalist system of production for profit, with its exploitation and impoverishment of the proletariat." (Socialists are very fond of these question-begging words.) I should say in this is the kernel of the whole socialist system of error.

What is this surplus value?

It is "the difference between the cost of labour-power to the capitalist and the amount of labour-power he is able to extract from his workpeople."

Give an example.

Mr. Bax would say that, if John Smith works in a boot factory eight hours a day, with the produce of four hours' work he provides his own sustenance, the other four hours he is working for his employer. That second four hours' work is surplus value, which is "wrung" from him; or, in other words, he is "exploited" by the employer, who gets all that for nothing.

Have you anything to say to that?

I have several things to say. First, no account is taken of rent of factory, interest on cost of machinery, repairs, risk, and so on. Secondly, if Smith did not work some time for his employer, how is the employer to live? As his whole time is taken up in superintending his men, how could he live if all the produce goes to those men?

Can you give an "argumentum ad hominen"?

I can. Mr. Bax every day buys a loaf of bread for fourpence. But the value of it to him is more than that—say, fivepence.

How can you prove that?

When flour rises in price, the loaf goes up to fivepence, and Mr. Bax gives that rather than go without bread. So he "wrings" from the baker a pennyworth of bread which he has not paid for, for nothing—that is, he "exploits" the baker, which, as he knows better, is very naughty of Mr. Bax.

What is the baker's position?

To him, again, the cost of producing the loaf is less than fourpence—say, threepence. So he "wrings" from Mr. Bax a penny, for which he has given nothing—that is, he "exploits" Mr. Bax. But as things have now got pretty mixed, and there is an old saying, "Pull Bax, pull baker," we will leave them to settle it between them.

Have you a third objection?

I have—a practical test. If John Smith is not satisfied, let him leave the factory and work on his own account. The fact of his entering the factory shows that he feels he does better there.

But do not the machinery, organisation, and division of labour in the factory enable him to produce much more than if he worked on his own account?

They do; but the whole of that excess is created not by him, but by the brains and labour of his employer. If the workman claims any of that, he is exploiting his employer. If he is not satisfied still, let him start as an employer.

But how can he get the capital?

In the same way as his employer did, who probably began as a workman. The famous James Nasmyth, inventor of the steam hammer, began business with £60. John Smith could save this in three years by putting off marriage.

But do not workmen often do what you suggest?

Very often; and the results are instructive. In going about the smaller streets I have often been struck, and saddened, by noticing that a shop which two years ago bore the name of "Brown, Tailor," and a year ago "Jones, Fishmonger," is now "Robinson, Grocer."

What does that mean?
That in each case a hard-working man has saved money, started in business, and failed.

Why has he failed?
For one or all of many reasons—fixing on a bad situation; want of judgment of the quality of goods, want of a head for figures; want of the gift of managing men. Many men are good servants, but bad masters.

What proportion of these ventures fail?
An American economist puts it at nine-tenths.

Then it is not the fact, as Mr. Bax and all Socialists assume, that the profits of capital are large?
No. That is one of the delusions but for which Socialism would not have arisen. If you divide the total profits of capital by the number of capitalists, the quotient is small.

Are the profits steady?
Not at all. Many prosperous businesses have periods, sometimes of several years, when they make nothing, or even a loss, yet the workmen get their wages all the time.

It is in the foundations, then, that Socialism is so weak?
Yes. An Irishman might describe it as an economic house of cards, founded on mares' nests of sentiment.

You spoke of wages. What is that?
The share of the produce given to the workman. In lengthy processes this is advanced out of capital.

How is the amount of wages fixed?

Socialists, consistently with their erroneous measuring of value by the amount of labour a thing has cost, say that it is determined by the cost of subsistence of the labourer. That is called the "Iron Law of Wages."

Is this so?

Of course, wages cannot fall below what will support life. But as the subsistence of one man costs about as much as that of another, and the wages of one man are often a hundred times as much as those of another, there must be another determinant.

What postulate lies at the root of the Socialist definition?

The assumption that workmen always multiply improvidently, so that there are more workmen than there are places. Mr. Bax says: "The labourer is not really free. He must sell his labour-power in order to live, and, having no control over the means of production, cannot employ himself." All this implies a man who spends all his wages, and goes into the labour market without a penny.

Do you accept this?

No. I have shown that, if a man saves, he can employ himself, as happens every day. If, in addition, he has the gift of management, he can employ others as well.

What, then, do Socialists want?

They want a man who has not the gift of management and does not manage, to be paid as if he did; a man who has no risk, to be paid compensation for risk; a man who contributes no capital, to receive interest on capital.

What really governs wages?

The ratio between the amount of capital available to pay them and the number of men seeking work.

But is not the idea of a wages fund abandoned?

It is by many, but it is a quibble about words. When capital is abundant and men few, wages rise. When the case is reversed, they fall. An employer looks to recoup himself for his outgoings and get interest on his capital and return for his brains and risk.

Then an employer does not object to high wages?

Quite the contrary, if he gets a proportionate return, as is seen in America.

What, then, is the way to raise wages?

To have increased production by increased talent in the employer devising improvements in machinery and processes, and increased energy and industry in the workmen.

Then wages cannot be raised by combination?

Not permanently. If there are more men than there is employment for, they can only be prevented from competing, and so lowering wages, by devoting the extra wages those at work get to buying off the unemployed.

But do not Socialists propose to abolish the wages system?

They do. That means that capital is to be provided and risk born by the whole community, instead of by the persons who are interested in providing the first and avoiding the second.

But do not Socialists say that production would be increased under their system?

They do—quintupled. As success in production depends on abundance of capital and minute attention to details, they expect an increase under a system where no one would feel any compulsion to produce capital—that is, to save—and no one would have the special knowledge, or the time, or the stimulus, to supervise details.

But would not public officials do that?

They could not provide capital, which must come from the savings of private persons. As for supervision, *Quis custodiet ipsos custodes?* They would require supervising, and it is universal experience that public management is more costly than private, owing to no one in particular feeling bound to acquire the knowledge or to give the time.

Then it all comes to this, that Socialism presupposes a radical change in human nature?

Exactly.

But do not Socialists expect also a great saving in consumption?

They do, by co-operative housekeeping. But this, if voluntary, has nothing socialistic about it. It is largely practiced now.

By all classes of persons?

No. People who are comfortably off, and are either single or without young children, often live in hotels or boarding-houses, and get more for their money than if they lived alone.

Then are there two kinds of economy?

There are. If a person has only £90 a year, it is no use telling him that for a payment of £100 in an hotel he can get £120 worth of comfort. By living alone he might get £80 worth of comfort for his £90.

But could he not save proportionately by cooperative living on the smaller sum?

With difficulty, for people shrink from practising petty economies in public. Besides, it would destroy the feeling of home. Compulsory co-operative living, as in workhouses and shelters, is a miserable thing.

What does history say?

Mr. Bax gives an historical sketch, beginning with the astonishing statement that the condition of the mass of the people is not improved, and that the purchasing power of money has decreased. He acknowledges that primitive society was communistic, but calls the introduction of slavery a step towards Individualism.

But is there not a difference between Socialism and ancient slavery?

Yes. The chief or owner of old got a larger share of the produce than his slaves. Socialism proposes that he should still furnish the capital and management, but share equally with the slaves.

Do not Socialists assert that the serfs had rights in the land of which they have been wrongfully deprived?

They do, and attribute pauperism and the necessity for the Poor Law to that cause.

But have there not been, and are there not now, many small owners?

There are, and always have been; but their condition is not so superior to that of the wage-labourer as to support the Socialist contention. The fact that most of the statesmen or small owners of Cumberland have sold their property shows that they cannot have been very flourishing.

Do not Socialists attribute much of present-day evils to some ogre called the capitalist system, which they assert to be a modern invention?

They do. Mr. Bax defines it as "large bodies of labourers working together for a single employer, and for his profit."

When does he say this began?

About the middle of the sixteenth century.

Is this historically correct?

It is not. Stonehenge, the Coliseum, the pyramids, the palaces of Babylon, the temples of India, could not have been made without large bodies of men working together for a single man, and for his profit, certainly not for their own.

Then was this system the same as the modern capitalist system?

By no means, though it answers Mr. Bax's definition. The ancient labour was wholly unproductive, was solely to gratify the vanity of a despot, and was attended with frightful suffering. In the modern system the workers unless they are redundant, which is not the capitalists' fault, always earn a comfortable subsistence for themselves, and sometimes a profit for their employer.

Then the difference between ancient and modern capitalism is in favor of modern?
Entirely, as far as the workman is concerned.

But do the workmen acknowledge this?
They do, by their actions, whatever their words may be. In Australia, where land may be had for the asking, men prefer to stop in the towns and work for wages, showing that they think themselves better off as wage-earners.

To what do you attribute the Socialist delusion that the workmen are exploited?
To their failure to understand the difference between productive and unproductive labour.

Explain your meaning.
They argue that as a man now, owing to machinery, division of labour, and other improvements, can produce many times more wealth than before, his share ought to be proportionately greater.

Is not that correct?
It is true that a man can produce a much greater quantity of lace, wall-paper, and all the ornaments of life; but he cannot produce much more food. The purchasing power, therefore, of those who grow corn or meat—that is, the excess of what they produce over what they consume—is not much greater than it was.

What is the effect on the producers of comforts and luxuries?
Their produce is cheapened—that is, they have to give a greater amount of it for the same quantity of food.

Then what is the difference between the state of the ancient and modern workman?

The ancient workman perhaps had as much to eat, but he did not eat it with a fork, drink out of glass, sleep in cotton sheets, have glazed windows, wall papers and pictures, and a hundred such refinements.

But does not the employer make a large profit?

Sometimes, if he is clever and fortunate, a small profit on each workman will amount to a large fortune in time; but the average profit is not large.

Do not large concerns tend to increase in number and size?

Naturally, with increased population, capital, and concentration, men who have the gift of organization have a greater opportunity of forming what Mr. Bax calls "giant octopus-like combinations which promise to bring all the businesses of the world under the control of a mere handful of wealthy capitalists."

Are these great businesses likely to be permanent?

Seeing that they are created by the talent of one man, and that talent and energy are not always inherited, they have a tendency to decline when the founder dies.

How do Socialists propose to cure this evil, as they consider, of big concerns?

By making them bigger still—that is, handing them over to Government.

What effect would that have?

Government would have to make the present employers managers, as no one else would have the talent. If they were selfish before, making them State officials would not make them less so, and they would have larger opportunities of enriching themselves with less supervision. If they died, and there was no one to succeed them, ruin would follow.

Did you not say that Mr. Bax devotes a section of his work to Socialist ethics?

He does, asserting that Socialism has a special code of ethics, as each stage of society has. He gives a history, in which he strangely mixes up ethics and religion, saying that ethics had first for its object the welfare of the tribe. It then became introspective, and the object was a divinity. But ethics has always been rules of conduct, the result of experience, inherited and acquired, of the conduct that promotes human welfare. Its object was always the community. The Spartan cheerfully gave his life for the good of his tribe. But that was because he found that, if every Spartan bravely risked death, his individual chance of life was better than if he ran away. We find Englishmen today just as ready to sacrifice their lives when necessary as Spartans were, only Spartans had to do it oftener, because of the savage manners of the time. Ethics, therefore, develops with the development of society, and is not perfect yet, for most people regard a wrong done to one of lower social position to themselves as less blameworthy than if done to their equal. Religion, on the other hand, has always been a personal affair. Men have pictured to themselves an invisible being like themselves, but stronger, whom they sought to propitiate. At first they gave presents and sacrifices. When they became ethical, they imagined an ethical god who was pleased with virtuous conduct; but the idea that he likes sacrifice and fulsome adulation, like an Eastern King, still lingers.

Does Mr. Bax tell us what Individualist ethics is like?
He does. It is the theory of the Manchester school of *economics*—namely, the individual scramble for wealth, the cash nexus, and purely material relations, instead of sentiment between men.

That sounds very confused.
It is. Cobden and Bright were not noted as ethical teachers, though they were persons of eminently ethical conduct, and, when ethical questions were discussed, advocated a pure and lofty morality. But their fame rests on the economic doctrine they preached—that if each person or nation devoted his or its energies to those commodities which it could produce with least effort, and exchanged with others, all would enjoy the maximum of satisfaction with the minimum of exertion.

How does Mr. Bax sum up Socialist ethics?
It is enlightened selfishness, since, in some unexplained way, under Socialism the good of all will be the good of each—that is, things will be made pleasant all round, and duty will never entail a sacrifice.

Why, then, does not everyone become a Socialist?
Because, we are told, they are not "class-conscious"—that is, they do not realize that their interests are opposed to those of the class above them.

Then we have a direct confession that envy is the origin of Socialism.
We have.

What are the political views of Socialists?
They are, Mr. Bax says, Little Englanders. They would gladly unite with foreign workmen to ruin their own country if they could

thereby plunder their employers or upset the present arrangement of society.

What is their attitude towards co-operation and trade unionism?

They view them with favour, so far as they may be a step in the same direction.

How do they view real improvements—such as thrift, temperance, and Malthusianism?

They hate them, as enabling workmen to live more cheaply, and so tending to lower wages, starting from the false assumption that wages never rise above the cost of maintenance.

Then the way for workmen to raise their wages would be to drink champagne?

Just so, by similar reasoning.

But is the object of those who preach temperance, thrift, and prudence in marriage to make workmen spend less?

Not at all, but to spend their income so as to have a greater amount of comfort and well-being, and, by having a reserve, to be able to move to where wages are high, and not have their efficiency impaired by sickness or loss of work.

Having criticized the Socialist view, can you give a summary of the Individualist doctrine?

I can. Individualism means enlisting the natural tendencies of human nature on behalf of well-being, as we all do when we reward our children if they are good and punish them if disobedient, and as a workman avails himself of the natural forces of gravitation, friction, etc., to do his work with the least effort. It holds, with Jesus, that good and evil spring from the heart of man and thence affect his surroundings, so that the way to improve him is to deal with the cause, by persuasion, and not with the effect, by compulsion. It holds that social progress, like all natural healthy growths, is slow and that no forced and artificial effect is permanent. It holds that every action has indirect and remote effects as well as immediate ones, and that the former are generally more important. It holds that the State has no money but what it takes from the people. It holds that denunciation of the idle rich who have earned or lawfully acquired their riches accords ill with the proposal to pension a man at his prime whether he has earned his pension or not. It holds that imperfect instruments cannot turn out perfect work, however good the scheme. It holds that periodicity is the law of the universe, so that the only way to prosperity is to work hard while we have the chance and make hay while the sun shines. It points to the success of the Jews and of all brain workers who pursue this plan. It points out that the time of England's prosperity coincides with the reign of *laissez faire* and the complaints of German competition with the present system of socialist interference.

25. FROM *A TREATISE ON POLITICAL ECONOMY*

ANTOINE DESTUTT DE TRACY

A Treatise on Political Economy, trans. Thomas Jefferson (Georgetown, DC: W. A. Rind & Co., 1817)

Antoine Destutt de Tracy (1754–1836) was a French philosopher who coined the word "ideology"—a discipline devoted to tracing our ideas to their origins in sense experience. An important critic of Napoleon, Tracy developed an economic and social theory of individualism in considerable detail. Tracy's book, A Treatise on Political Economy, *was translated into English with the assistance of Thomas Jefferson, after which it became a popular textbook on free-market economics in southern universities. In the following passage, we see a brief but insightful analysis of the nature of society.*

Society is purely and solely a continual series of exchanges. It is never any thing else, in any epoch of its duration, from its commencement the most unformed, to its greatest perfection. And this is the greatest eulogy we can give to it, for exchange is an admirable transaction, in which the two contracting parties always both gain; consequently society is an uninterrupted succession of advantages, unceasingly renewed for all its members. . . .

. . .[A]n exchange is a transaction in which the two contracting parties both gain. Whenever I make an exchange freely, and without constraint, it is because I desire the thing I receive more than that I give; and, on the contrary, he with whom I bargain desires what I offer more than that which he renders me. When I give my labour for wages it is because I esteem the wages more than what I should have been able to produce by labouring for myself; and he who pays me prizes more the services I render him than what he gives me in return. When I give a measure of wheat for a measure of wine, it is because I have a superabundance of food and nothing to drink, and he with whom I treat is in the contrary case. When several of us agree to execute any labour whatsoever in common, whether to defend ourselves against an enemy, to destroy noxious animals, to preserve ourselves from the ravages of the sea, of an inundation, of a contagion, or even to make a bridge or a road, it is because each of us prefers the particular utility which will result to him from it, to what he would have been able to do for himself during the same time. We are all satisfied in all these species of exchanges; every one finds his advantage in the arrangement proposed.

26. FROM *ASPECTS OF THE RISE OF ECONOMIC INDIVIDUALISM*

H. M. ROBERTSON

Aspects of the Rise of Economic Individualism: A Criticism of Max Weber and His School (London: Cambridge University Press, 1933)

The economic historian H. M. Robertson was senior lecturer in economics at the University of Cape Town. The excerpt reprinted here is the conclusion of Aspects of the Rise of Economic Individualism: A Criticism of Max Weber and His School. *Contrary to Weber, who traced the spirit of capitalism to the rise of Puritanism, Robertson attributes the rise of capitalism and economic individualism to an emerging secularism.*

The chief factor in the triumph of bourgeois liberalism was the factor of economic development which made the bourgeoisie important. It came into its own as a secular force. The rise of bourgeois morality in England as a substitute for religion was not the product of Puritanism. In Catholic France one found preachers complaining in the eighteenth century that a "gospel of worldly probity, in which is comprised all the duties of reason and religion" had arisen "on the ruins of the gospel of Jesus Christ"; and that the bourgeois preferred to be known as *honnête homme* rather than as a good Christian. The Churches in each country had been unable in the end, in spite of all their efforts, to assimilate the class of self-made men. The decline of the Churches in England as witnesses to a Christian code of social ethics was not due to a Puritan belief that "the Lorde was with

Joseph, and he was a luckie felowe". It was due to the unwilling-
ness of a rising bourgeoisie to be bound by what it considered to
be antiquated rules.

Even so, there is no reason to decry too violently the new bourgeois individualism with its profane, not Puritan origins. It was
not a mere product of greed. It inculcated a belief in honour and
justice, it believed firmly in justice, thought that independently
of all religion there was implanted in man a love of justice, and
on this it built. It did not ask for liberty for men to indulge their
anti-social greed. It asked liberty for them to look after themselves in accordance with the rules which life and business both
require to be respected and the observance of which was thought
to be innate to man's nature; the rules of respecting contracts and
of not doing to others what one would not have done to oneself.
It did not ask for economic freedom because it believed that
man's spirit of emulation raised an antithesis between the common and the private good, but because it disbelieved it.

It believed that man was rational enough to prefer justice to
injustice, and that free competition would be more efficacious in
promoting just dealing (on the assumption that, in general, men
had a preference for justice whilst any who had not would find it
bad policy to indulge their love of cheating) than restrictions
based on the assumption that all men were rogues.

It was not from greed that the new individualism attacked the
restrictions on forestalling and regrating. It was because it
believed that free competition would see the market better and
more cheaply supplied. It was not greed that silently broke down
the restrictions on usury; it was a recognition that the usury
restrictions did not work as they were intended. It was not mere
greed that protested against the restrictions on foreign trade
formed by the existence of the chartered companies. It was a just

protest against injurious monopolies. It was a demand that regard should be had for the realities of things, not words; that sentimentalism should not be allowed to mask the grasping selfishness of the corporations which were impairing the well-being of the country they were supposed to serve. Self-interest played a part in promoting the rise of economic individualism, but not the only part—even when it is recognised that much apparently disinterested reasoning may be merely the rationalisation of selfish motives. The problem must not be simplified too far.

Some day the tangled antecedents of the doctrine of economic individualism may be unravelled. But they will not be unravelled by concentrating on religion, or by search for the clues in greed, selfishness and the self-centred righteousness of men who work hard in their "calling". Perhaps those who are interested in the problems of the rise of modern capitalism and economic individualism will turn more to secular channels for enlightenment. The chief school of the economists of the sixteenth and seventeenth centuries was business experience. Re-explore after them the commercial field in which they worked, and one cannot fail to pick up some indications of the growth of their philosophy. This is not the only field for research—law and literature, philosophy and politics, all sorts of considerations are relevant to the problem. But it is a most promising field, and one which has been unduly neglected.

RECOMMENDED READING

Arieli, Yehoshua. *Individualism and Nationalism in American Ideology.* Cambridge, MA: Harvard University Press, 1964.

Berman, Marshall. *The Politics of Authenticity: Radical Individualism and the Emergence of Modern Society.* London: Verso, 2009. First published 1970 by Atheneum.

Gurevich, Aaron. *The Origins of European Individualism.* Translated by Katharine Judelson. Oxford, UK, and Cambridge, MA: Blackwell, 1995.

Heller, Thomas C., Morton Sosna, and David E. Wellbery, with Arnold I. Davidson, Ann Swidler, and Ian Watt. *Reconstructing Individualism: Autonomy, Individuality, and the Self in Western Thought.* 1986. Reprint, Stanford: Stanford University Press, 1988.

Keohane, Nannerl O. *Philosophy and the State in France: The Renaissance to the Enlightenment.* Princeton: Princeton University Press, 1980.

Lukes, Steven. *Individualism.* Key Concepts in the Social Sciences. Oxford, UK: Basil Blackwell, 1973.

Macfarlane, Alan. *The Origins of English Individualism: The Family, Property and Social Transition.* Oxford, UK: Basil Blackwell, 1978.

Martin, John Jeffries. *Myths of Renaissance Individualism.* London: Palgrave Macmillan, 2004.

Martin, Raymond and John Barresi. *The Rise and Fall of Soul and Self: An Intellectual History of Personal Identity.* New York: Columbia University Press, 2006.

Morris, Colin. *The Discovery of The Individual 1050–1200.* Medieval Academy Reprints for Teaching 19. Toronto, Buffalo, and London: University of Toronto Press, 1987.

Nisbet, Robert. *The Social Philosophers: Community & Conflict in Western Thought.* New York: Thomas Y. Crowell, 1973.

Presley, Sharon, and Crispin Sartwell. *Exquisite Rebel: The Essays of Voltairine de Cleyre—Anarchist, Feminist, Genius.* Albany: State University of New York Press, 2005.

Reichert, William O. *Partisans of Freedom: A Study in American Anarchism.* Bowling Green, OH: Bowling Green University Popular Press, 1976.

Schumpeter, Joseph A. *Capitalism, Socialism and Democracy.* 3rd ed. New York and Evanston, IL: Harper & Row, 1950.

Sears, Hal D. *The Sex Radicals: Free Love in High Victorian America.* Lawrence, KS: Regents Press of Kansas, 1977.

Seigel, Jerrold. *The Idea of the Self: Thought and Experience in Western Europe Since the Seventeenth Century.* 2005. Reprint, Cambridge: Cambridge University Press, 2007.

Simmel, Georg. "Individual and Society in Eighteenth- and Nineteenth-Century Views of Life." Chap. 4 in *The Sociology of Georg Simmel.* Translated, edited, and introduction written by Kurt H. Wolff. New York: Free Press, 1950.

———. "Freedom and the Individual." Chap. 15 in *Georg Simmel On Individuality and Social Forms: Selected Writings.* Edited and introduction written by Donald N. Levine. Chicago and London: University of Chicago Press, 1971.

Smith, George H. "Individualism." Chap. 9 in *The System of Liberty: Themes in the History of Classical Liberalism.* Cambridge: Cambridge University Press, 2013.

Stone, Lawrence. "The Growth of Affective Individualism." Chap. 6 in *The Family, Sex and Marriage in England 1500–1800.* New York: Harper, 1979. First published 1977 by Penguin Books.

Ullmann, Walter. *Medieval Foundations of Renaissance Humanism.* London: Elek Books, 1977.

———. *The Individual and Society in the Middle Ages.* Baltimore: Johns Hopkins University Press, 1966.

Watt, Ian. *The Rise of the Novel: Studies in Defoe, Richardson and Fielding.* Berkeley and Los Angeles: University of California Press, 1959.

INDEX

vices and, 108
women's rights and, 91–92
Bonald, Louis-Gabriel-Amboise
de, 15
bourgeoisie
moral code of, 223
and rise of economic individuality, 222–24
Burckhardt, Jacob, 8, 19–22
Burke, Edmund, 6–7, 16

Callero, Peter L., 2–3
Calvinism, 45
capital
availability to small businesses, 207
socialist definition of, 202–3
capitalism
growth of corporations in, 215
socialist definition of, 213
See also competition; individualism, economic
capitalists, as class, socialist
theory on, 202
A Catechism of Individualism (Wilson), 191–219
Catholic Church
and social order, 6–7, 14–15
suppression of individual
thought by, 183–84, 186
See also Christianity
Chapman, John, 29
character, as expression of individual impulses, 43
Chartists, 177
children, rearing of, 133–34
China, cultural stagnation of,
56, 57–58

Christianity
ideal of self-development in,
46
and rise of individualism,
24–25
See also Catholic Church
Cicero, 66
circumstance, tyranny of, 77–78
The City of God (Augustine of
Hippo), 73–74
civic virtues, individualism and,
8
civilization
advance of, and refinement
of individuality, 34–36
and loss of instinct for freedom, 182
See also progress, social
The Civilization of the Renaissance
in Italy (Burckhardt), 19–
22
class-consciousness, and socialism, 217
classical liberalism, 12
de Cleyre, Voltairine, 77–79
clothing, conformity and, 56–
57, 62
cohabitation, advocates of, 87–
93, 102
common good
benefits of economic individualism for, 201
as motive for action, 118
right to property and, 147
self-interest rightly understood and, 11
trade as contribution to, 151
vagueness of term, 2–3

ABOUT THE EDITORS

George H. Smith writes a weekly column for Libertarianism.org. His fourth book, *The System of Liberty: Themes in the History of Classical Liberalism*, was published in 2013 by Cambridge University Press.

Marilyn Moore has a PhD in English literature. She is an adjunct professor of English and Rhetoric at Triton College (Illinois) and also works as a freelance editor.

CATO INSTITUTE

Founded in 1977, the Cato Institute is a public policy research foundation dedicated to broadening the parameters of policy debate to allow consideration of more options that are consistent with the principles of limited government, individual liberty, and peace. To that end, the Institute strives to achieve greater involvement of the intelligent, concerned lay public in questions of policy and the proper role of government.

The Institute is named for Cato's Letters, libertarian pamphlets that were widely read in the American Colonies in the early 18th century and played a major role in laying the philosophical foundation for the American Revolution.

Despite the achievement of the nation's Founders, today virtually no aspect of life is free from government encroachment. A pervasive intolerance for individual rights is shown by government's arbitrary intrusions into private economic transactions and its disregard for civil liberties. And while freedom around the globe has notably increased in the past several decades, many countries have moved in the opposite direction, and most governments still do not respect or safeguard the wide range of civil and economic liberties.

To address those issues, the Cato Institute undertakes an extensive publications program on the complete spectrum of policy issues. Books, monographs, and shorter studies are commissioned to examine the federal budget, Social Security, regulation, military spending, international trade, and myriad other issues. Major policy conferences are held throughout the year, from which papers are published thrice yearly in the Cato Journal. The Institute also publishes the quarterly magazine Regulation.

In order to maintain its independence, the Cato Institute accepts no government funding. Contributions are received from foundations, corporations, and individuals, and other revenue is generated from the sale of publications. The Institute is a nonprofit, tax-exempt, educational foundation under Section 501(c)3 of the Internal Revenue Code.

CATO INSTITUTE
1000 Massachusetts Ave., N.W.
Washington, D.C. 20001
www.cato.org